ROBERT LOUIS STEVENSON IN CALIFORNIA

THE LITERARY WEST SERIES

BY THE SAME AUTHOR:
Brother Whale
Lahaina — Royal Capital of Hawaii
Hawaii the Volcano State

SAN FRANCISCO

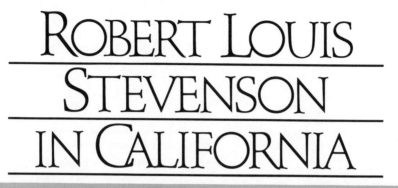

ROBERT LOUIS STEVENSON IN CALIFORNIA

A REMARKABLE COURTSHIP

BY ROY NICKERSON

CHRONICLE BOOKS

LIBRARY OF CONGRESS CATALOGING IN
PUBLICATION DATA

Nickerson, Roy.
Robert Louis Stevenson in California.
(The Literary West series)
Bibliography: p. 115.
Includes index.
1. Stevenson, Robert Louis, 1850–1894 –
Homes and haunts – California.
2. Authors, Scottish – 19th century –
Biography. 3. California – Biography.
I. Title. II. Series.
PR5494.N5 1982 828'.809 [B] 82-9643
ISBN 0-87701-246-6

BOOK AND COVER DESIGN
Howard Jacobsen

COMPOSITION
Sara Schrom, Type by Design

EDITING
Sylvia E. Stein

CHRONICLE BOOKS
870 Market Street
San Francisco, California 94102

The author wishes to acknowledge the
sources of material quoted:

Lloyd Osbourne, An Intimate Portrait
of R.L.S. Copyright 1924 Charles
Scribner's Sons; copyright renewed 1952
Charles Scribner's Sons. Reprinted with
permission.

Nellie Van de Grift Sanchez, "In California with Robert Louis Stevenson,"
from Scribner's Magazine, October 1916.
Copyright 1916 by Charles Scribner's
Sons; copyright renewed 1944 by
Charles Scribner's Sons. Reprinted with
permission.

Excerpts from The Violent Friend: The
Story of Mrs. Robert Louis Stevenson by
Margaret Mackay. Copyright ©1968 by
Margaret Mackay. Reprinted by per-
mission of Doubleday & Company, Inc.

Americans and the California Dream:
1850–1915 by Kevin Starr. Copyright
©1973 by Oxford University Press, Inc.
Reprinted by permission.

PHOTO AND ILLUSTRATION CREDITS

Colton Hall Museum, Monterey:
page 25.

Harrison Memorial Library, Carmel:
page 54.

Roy Nickerson: pages 37, 42, 98, 113.

Silverado Museum, St. Helena: pages
16, 103.

Stevenson House, Monterey: front
cover, pages 10, 46, 82, 84, 108.

Michael Schoepp: page 55.

Contents

PREFACE

IT SEEMS IMPOSSIBLE THAT
there are some people who might not immediately recognize the initials RLS. Yet I suppose there are a great many. There was a time when I would have asked rhetorically, "Who today has not been raised on *A Child's Garden of Verses, Treasure Island,* or *Kidnapped?*" I certainly was, and often with the maternal admonition to appreciate the fact that RLS "was a fellow Scot." Mother came from Nova Scotia, and those before her, from Inverness, Scotland, and the other tribes that people my personal background in the United Kingdom have long been relegated to cobweb-covered pigeonholes. To live today when she would have been allowed to list her name as Ross-Nickerson would have delighted her.

Some time ago, when I first met Silverado Museum Curator Ellen Shaffer, she was lamenting what she felt to be a dramatic deterioration in the teaching of reading skills these days . . . and what she feared was the accompanying drop in awareness of RLS simply because youngsters are no longer being exposed as much to his works by teachers or parents. And yet a short time ago she delightedly told me of the number of people or organizations that had recently contacted her for help in preparing a variety of television, book and magazine projects concerning RLS.

"Stevenson seems to be riding the crest of the wave!" she exclaimed.

In scouting around California to research this book I have found nothing but intense interest in both Stevenson the man and his work—and anything left behind that he may have touched. Between the Stevenson House in Monterey and the Silverado Museum in St. Helena, he is well represented. One can tread his footsteps all over town in Monterey; in St. Helena one may look into a mirror that has not only reflected back RLS's image, but that of Sir Walter Scott and his ilk as well.

Among the people I wish to thank for their help, the first three, out of conscience, can only be listed alphabetically: Robert W. Reese, district historian for the California Department of Parks and Recreation, headquartered in Monterey; Ellen Shaffer, indefatigable curator of the Silverado Museum, St. Helena; and scholarly Roger G. Swearingen of San Francisco, a member of the University of California faculty.

Among many others whose assistance and patience were invaluable are both the front desk and reference librarians of the Harrison Memorial Library, Carmel; the reference librarians at the Monterey Public Library who guided me through the stacks of the California Room; anonymous workers who sent me copies of materials requested from the California State Library, Sacramento; the staff at the Colton Hall Museum, Monterey; Michael Schoepp, who chauffeured me all over Silverado country without complaint and helped with the photos; and Carmel patroness of the arts Alexandra Morrow, who always seemed to find a solution, no matter how complicated the problem.

Robert Louis Stevenson in California

RLS IN 1887 WEARING A MOURNING BAND IN
MEMORY OF HIS FATHER.

Robert Louis Stevenson in California

I
INTRODUCTION:
DRAMATIS
PERSONAE

ROBERT LOUIS STEVENSON'S
life was a drama from start to finish. It was a drama of very real, although sometimes self-imposed, suffering; it was also a drama of intrigue, of triumphs, of passion and ultimately of tragedy. We remember him best for his triumphs—his writings. All of this also tells us that by nature he was a romantic; only a romantic could have wanted to live the life he lived.

Years after his death, his sister-in-law, Nellie Van de Grift Sanchez, wrote of him: "In the year 1879 there remained one spot in practical America where the spirit of romance still lingered, though even there she stood a-tiptoe, ready to take wing into the mists of the Pacific. It seems fitting that it should have been at that place, Monterey, California, that I first knew Robert Louis Stevenson, prince of romance . . ."

This book concerns itself only with Stevenson's time in California, a time usually referred to as the turning point in his career as a writer; I will, of course, touch briefly on the outcome of the California influence on the Scottish writer and what happened to him after he traveled on.

Because I start this story of Robert Louis Stevenson when he had already lived more than half his life, it is important to know who were the leading characters in his drama. Those he met in California will, of course, introduce themselves. Here briefly are the vital statistics of those people I will start to deal with almost immediately, including the star, listed the way they appear in the text.

RLS:

Robert Louis Stevenson was born November 13, 1850, in Edinburgh, Scotland. He was the only son of a highly successful engineer, *Thomas Stevenson*, and *Margaret Isabella Balfour*. He was subsequently christened into the strict Presbyterian Church, against which he later rebelled violently, as Robert Lewis Balfour Stevenson. David Daiches writes: ". . . the child did not long remain 'Lewis,' for his Tory father took a violent dislike to a radical named Lewis and changed the spelling of his son's name to prevent even an orthographical association with the man. But, though spelt in the French manner, the name was always pronounced with the final 's' sounded." And RLS himself dropped the Balfour when he started writing.

According to Rosaline Masson, RLS must have taken after his mother, who was "delicate, with a tendency to chest weakness and nervous troubles." RLS had been born at No. 8 Howard Place, Edinburgh, but the family soon moved to 1 Inverleith Terrace. Mrs. Masson writes that when the boy was two, the family moved to even grander quarters at 17 Heriot Row. "Evidently it was damp! The first thing that happened was that the new tenants' baby had a severe attack of the croup; and from then onwards every year brought its attack of some illness, weakening the little frame." According to Margaret Mackay, when he was a child, Stevenson's immediate family referred to him as Smout, which means a small salmon or small fry. He took a dislike to the nickname as he approached adolescence and finally levied a fine of one penny on everyone who called him that. He was more usually called Lew, then after the name change, Louis. The name Bob was already in use by his older (and favorite) cousin, Robert Stevenson.

As he progressed into his teens, rebelled against his church and convention in general, took to Edinburgh's houses of prostitution and decided he wanted to become a writer (not necessarily in that order), he affected long hair and Bohemian attire, which earned him the sobriquet about town of "Velvet Coat." Mrs. Mackay has assembled this word picture of the mature RLS: "He was five feet ten, with incredibly fine bones. . . . His face was oval, with high cheekbones, an aquiline nose like his mother's, a deceptively ruddy colour, fair hair that darkened with the years, an eloquent mouth 'a little tricksy and mocking,' and great brown eyes of a penetrating brilliance, set exceptionally far apart."

RLS's father had hoped his son would follow in the family profession. Mrs. Masson writes: "His father, Thomas Stevenson, had been born and brought up in Edinburgh, one of the 13 children of the famous engineer of the Bell Rock Lighthouse, Robert Stevenson. It was with this Robert Stevenson, RLS's grandfather, that Sir Walter Scott went on the voyage in 1814 with the Lighthouse Commissioners, that gave him [Scott] his material for *The Pirate*." RLS, however, had no such inclination, and his father agreed to send him through the University to read law. He got his degree, but never practiced. He announced to a heartbroken but resigned father that he wished to be "a mere scribbler." He continued to live off a family allowance that was augmented from time to time so that he could travel to the South of France or to Davos, depending on the current advice of his doctors, to rejuvenate his sickly lungs, which regularly damaged themselves with severe hemorrhaging.

Mrs. Masson, who was writing a mere 24 years after the death of RLS, summed up her subject this way: "Louis Stevenson was abnormal, both in mind and body. He was an invalid trying to live the life of an ordinary youth in a climate that is not adapted for invalids; and he was a genius, trying to feel his way in a world that is not adapted to geniuses, because it is ruled by laws and customs made for, and made by, very average intellects."

FANNY:

Frances Matilda Vandegrift was born March 10, 1840, in the frontier town of Indianapolis, Indiana. At age 16, she became Mrs. Samuel C. Osbourne, at which time she changed the spelling of her maiden name to the more aristocratic Van de Grift. She was eventually to become best known as Fanny Stevenson, but her future husband was not born until she was already a very active 10-year-old. Fanny was born of mixed Dutch, Swedish, and English colonial parents. Her mother is said to be a descendant of the English navigator, Capt. James Cook.

All her biographies make much of the fact that she was dark-complexioned and had curly hair. Noted Edward Rice: "Her daughter-in-law, Katharine Durham Osbourne, a woman who hated Fanny for unfathomable reasons, wrote, 'she belonged to the childhood of the race—the first beginning of civilization—in some dark-skinned peoples.'" (The "unfathomable reasons" were reciprocated; Fanny's son, Lloyd, married Katharine after the death of RLS but eventually divorced her; the entire family had taken an instant dislike to her. She later wrote what is probably the most unreliable book ever published about RLS, whom she never met.) One rumor also was that Fanny's mother had been secretly married and divorced from a Creole. Despite the number of racist remarks made about Fanny, Ellen Shaffer, curator of the Silverado Museum in St. Helena, California, has the most sensible explanation of Fanny's "swarthy Gypsy beauty: "Fanny was of Dutch extraction, which brings in a Moorish strain."

Fanny grew up to be fiercely independent and extremely talented. The home in which she was born was next door to the Second Presbyterian Church of Indianapolis, of which the minister was the Rev. Henry Ward Beecher. He baptized her at the age of two into the same strict religion as her future husband. One day when Fanny was 16 the Governor of Indiana came to a public function she also attended, but the one who caught her eye was the Governor's secretary, Lt. Sam Osbourne. The attraction was mutual and they were married December 4, 1857. Nine months later a honeymoon child, Isobel, was born. Sam was a ladies' man and neither marriage nor parenthood calmed him down.

Although she wanted to study art and wanted to write, Fanny eventually accompanied her husband to a Nevada mining camp where he had short-lived work and where she learned to roll her own cigarettes—a shocking accomplishment for a lady of the post–Civil War years! In 1868 the marriage produced a second child, Samuel Lloyd, and in 1871, a second son, Hervey. In between periods of family togetherness, however, Sam's philandering got to the point where Fanny decided it was useless to make a pretense of married life as a family. She decided in 1875 to follow her heart's desire to Paris and study art. With the aid of a continuing allowance from her husband, she took her three children, and after getting over the shock of learning that women had art classes separate from men, she enrolled at Atelier des Dames while a governess looked after the children. She was thrilled when the teacher assigned another student to familiarize her with the class procedures; the fellow student was Amy, sister of Louisa May Alcott and one of her *Little Women*.

Hervey became ill and it was obvious he would not live. Sam Osbourne arrived just in time to see the lad before he died of scrofulous tuberculosis on April 5, 1876. Their other son, Lloyd, now appeared physically and emotionally drained by the events and a doctor advised Fanny to take him to the quiet of the countryside. Inquiries after a suitable place they could also afford took them to Grèz, a village on the Loing River over which spanned a small bridge artists loved to paint. It was some 60 miles from Paris. Sam remained only briefly, promising to send money now and again.

They lived in a spartan, family-style hotel where everyone sat around the same table for meals. It was a hotel favored by Bohemians, and it was visited regularly by an Irish poet, British travelers and would-be writers, as well as Continental artists. As the season approached, one Robert Stevenson arrived, and Fanny thought he was quite the most attractive man she had ever met. But Bob Stevenson, like everyone else, only replied, "Wait until my cousin Louis gets here!" Louis—RLS—soon did arrive and created quite an amount of excitement. Not only was he unusual in appearance and dress, but he was one of history's wittiest conversationalists. As Bob Stevenson continued to ignore politely Fanny's interest in him, she transferred her attentions to RLS. RLS apparently was immediately struck by her, and his parents eventually learned, to their utter horror, that he was interested in a woman who was not only older—which was a trait they were now used to—but married at that!

The Stevensons eventually went back to Scotland and England and Fanny and her children returned to Paris. But the next summer all parties again returned to Grèz. RLS wrote and Fanny painted; daughter Isobel studied art; son Lloyd took a liking to "Luly"—he could not yet pronounce "Louis"—and Sam Osbourne sent a note saying he was tired of paying for a family *in absentia*.

Fanny and the children returned to the San Francisco Bay Area in what was apparently a final attempt to save the marriage. It

LLOYD AT 11, AS DRAWN BY SISTER BELLE.

Robert Louis Stevenson in California

didn't work. Almost two years after they had last seen each other, one of her sporadic letters to RLS expressed utter anguish at the way she was living and she told him her despair had driven her to physical illness. RLS, without immediately telling his parents and against the advice of his friends, scraped together what cash he could and went to America by the cheapest transportation possible: an immigrant ship, the *Devonia*.

BELLE:

Isobel Osbourne Strong Field was the first of Sam and Fanny Osbourne's three children. She shared her mother's dark complexion and as a child was quite self-conscious about it. Her mother one day advised her to "be like Sarah Bernhardt." If she considered her darkness a flaw, she should treat it as a special mark of beauty. Belle was born in September of 1858, but the joy of parenthood did little to cool off the amorous adventures of Sam Osbourne. Fanny left the Indiana home for California almost immediately.

In her autobiography, *This Life I've Loved*, Belle records that she first met her future husband, Joe Strong, when she was 14. It was also a day she saw one of San Francisco's fabled characters: "We [a girlfriend and she] had seen Emperor Norton come on board [the Oakland–San Francisco ferry], the crowds making way for him quite seriously and bowing as he took his seat. I never saw anyone laugh at or ridicule Emperor Norton though he was an eccentric figure in his rusty uniform with gold epaulettes, cocked hat and feather, belt and sword, and his knobby cane . . . a poor and demented man that all San Francisco guarded and humored. He had been a respected citizen who lost his fortune on the stock exchange." Such was the era in which Belle passed her adolescence, and it was that same day and aboard the same ferry that "we noticed that a couple of young men were looking at us with interest. Demurely, out of the corner of my eye I discovered that the taller one was making a sketch of me."

It was some three years later, after time in France with her mother and two brothers and the traumatic return to California before – and again by chance – she ran into the artist again and married him. The marriage lasted 14 years, when Belle decided she could no longer cope with life with an alcoholic. They were divorced. Much of the rest of her life was determined by the fact she and her mother inherited RLS's estate and fame. Both went to live in the Santa Barbara area after the San Francisco earthquake of 1906. After marrying Ned Field she continued her interests in art and writing, continued to be an object of curiosity because she became the sole survivor of RLS's family circle. She died in Santa Barbara June 26, 1953, at the age of 94.

SAM OSBOURNE:

Hovering in the background of RLS's life from the time he met Fanny Osbourne and her children at Grèz in 1876 was Samuel C. Osbourne, Fanny's first husband and the father of the two surviving children who were to become RLS's stepson and stepdaughter. Long after the end of the relationship between Sam and Fanny, there was always the indistinct influence that guided the attitudes of all four.

He had been born in Kentucky almost four years before Fanny and was a descendant of Daniel Boone. He had become a lieutenant in the Indiana Militia, then secretary to that state's governor. A law graduate, he was described as tall, handsome, blond and sporting a Van Dyke beard.

Sam and Fanny were married December 4, 1857. Fanny was 17 and Sam, 20. Four years later he joined the Indiana regiment in the Civil War, won a commission as a captain, but had no heart for war and returned to Indiana to that day's equivalent of the National Guard. Mrs. Mackay writes that this was not because he was a coward, but because he couldn't stick to anything for long. Next Sam sold his wife's family property to finance a trip to California, via the Panama Canal, and eventually he sent for her.

They ended up in a Nevada mining camp where Fanny pretty much had to learn to fend for herself. She proved to be a gifted home-maker by improvisation, but Sam's fortunes did not pan out any gold or other precious item, and they moved on to Virginia City, Nevada. Next the lure of silver called and Sam went off with a friend to pros-pect. When word came back that Sam had been killed by Indians, Fanny and Belle went off to San Francisco.

Sam, however, had not been killed, and he returned to Fanny and sired their first son, Samuel Lloyd—called Lloyd after the divorce and known thus to history. This was in April, 1868. Sam continued to succumb to his weakness for women other than his wife, but returned to the Oakland home from time to time, interrupt-ting Fanny's art lessons in San Francisco, where she earned a silver

medal for a drawing of Venus de Milo and where she met an art in-
structor who, along with his wife, was destined to become close
friends of Fanny and her second husband, RLS: Virgil Williams was
the artist. Belle shared the classes. In 1871 ill-starred Hervey was
born. Again, the arrival of a child in the family failed to make a home-
body out of Sam.

Both his children write lovingly of him, and young Belle and
Samuel Lloyd dwell on his "gaiety" and his thoughtfulness. As children, they did not see the unpleasantness between their mother and
father, but were only happy to see him return from his wanderings.
Lloyd took to RLS from the start and perhaps was too young to see
any question of rivalry. He was the first to learn that RLS was going
to marry his mother, and he immediately rejoiced at the prospect.
Belle, years later, told Elsie Noble Caldwell, who wrote *Last Witness for Robert Louis Stevenson* in 1960, "Maybe my mother saw in
this contrast to my father (with RLS) the security from infidelity that
wrecked their marriage. At any rate she was happy when he was
near, and I, standing in awe of her inflexible decisions, had no hope-
ful moments that she would not marry this penniless foreigner. At
seventeen I would sit in judgment to be regretted in shame for the
rest of my life!" She was referring to the fact that she never took to
RLS the same way Lloyd did. It was several years later, in Sydney,
Australia, when the dying Stevenson pleaded for a family to remain
with him at his last home in Samoa, that she suddenly understood
how unjust her resentment toward RLS was, how deeply he loved
her as Fanny's daughter, and how genuinely he wanted her to remain
within the family circle that he headed. Like a clap of thunder the
realization struck her; a tearful embrace with RLS ensued; and
instead of going off on her own as she had at that moment intended
to do, she happily returned to Samoa.

Sam Osbourne died in 1881, apparently a suicide. He had obtained a highly respectable job as court recorder in San Francisco.
One day he simply disappeared. His children always stated that he
had obviously been killed by robbers. Some time later, however,
clothing identified as his was found at the edge of San Francisco Bay.

JOE STRONG:

Joseph Dwight Strong, Jr., was born in Westport, Connecticut, in
1852. The senior Strong was a Congregational minister who went to

Hawaii as a missionary soon after young Joe's birth. He and his sister, Elizabeth, three years younger, lived their childhood in Hawaii. The Strong family then moved to Oakland, California.

While still a teenager, Joe demonstrated exceptional talent as an artist. As Belle's biography records, his first impulse upon meeting her was to sketch her. They exchanged names and addresses after that first meeting, and Joe later asked Belle to come to his formal studio so he could paint her portrait. "Much to my amazement," Belle later wrote, "my mother gave me permission to go to the studio. . . . It was a tiny room up two flights of stairs, on Broadway in Oakland, and there Joe painted a small picture of me, and his friend Reginald Birch made a pen and ink drawing. It was he who later illustrated Little Lord Fauntleroy so delightfully. Though I heard from them occasionally, I didn't see Joe Strong again for four years." That, of course, was because she had gone to Europe with her mother.

Joe, too, went to Europe, but to Munich, Germany, far from the forests of Fontainebleau. Just before his first meeting with Belle, a portrait he had done of the mayor of Oakland had gained such public praise that a fund was raised to send him off to study under two master artists named Piloty and Wagner.

He returned to Oakland in 1877 and became a highly successful portrait artist. He became active in the Bohemian Club and gained rewarding commissions from his fellow members. He eventually decided to follow the art crowd to Monterey, where Jules Tavernier is credited with having founded the art colony—dividing his time between San Francisco and Monterey—and that is where Joe next saw Belle. Fanny had gone there with her children to think things out away from Oakland, where her husband continued to pursue the ladies and where she even had a run-in with one of them who had the nerve to attempt to call on her at their home. She knew divorce was the only answer; the problem was that, in the 1870s, divorce was unthinkable in respectable circles.

It was here that Belle once again came in contact with Joe, and they eloped from there. They moved to San Francisco, partly to escape a furious Fanny, who was in the process of arranging a "more suitable marriage" for her daughter. Belle's father helped them to get established. Joe's work eventually attracted the attention of Claus Spreckels, the sugar king, who commissioned him to go to Hawaii to do some paintings for him there. Joe welcomed the opportunity to return to the Islands, and he and his talented wife were soon well established there.

In those days there were two social circles to which one could aspire, the "missionary group" and the "royal circle." The Strongs opted for the royal circle and soon became fast friends with King Kalakaua and his court. Belle did artwork for him, including the design of a decoration the King bestowed as rewards for service to the Throne. Some time later she was the surprised recipient of the very decoration she had designed because, during the uprising against the King in 1883, she was able to smuggle some messages to His Majesty that helped thwart the short-lived rebellion.

The Strongs had two children, Austin and another boy who died in Hawaii. As talented as Joe was as an artist, he had other weaknesses that caused periodic separations to take the cure. He was, it appears, a hopeless alcoholic who filched the household money to pay for booze. When Belle eventually found a cache of unpaid bills and learned that they were living on the kindness of a number of purveyors, Joe went off the first time to dry out while she went to work to pay the debts. Years later, when they were living with the Stevensons in Samoa, it happened again. Fanny's diary entry of December 23, 1892, sums up the rest: "My diary has been long neglected. About the time I stopped writing we found Joe Strong out in various misdeeds, robbing the cellar and store-room at night with false keys; in revenge, when he found that he had been discovered, he went round to all our friends in Apia and spread slanders abut Belle. We turned him away, and applied for a divorce for Belle, which was got with no difficulty, as he had been living with a native woman of Apia as his wife . . ."

RLS took such a voilent dislike to Joe that he cut him out of a photo that showed himself, Lloyd Osbourne, and some horses and skillfully patched it back together so that the deletion was never noticed.

Joe returned to San Francisco to resume a successful career as a portrait artist. He died there April 5, 1899. I find no record about his other sister, but Elizabeth lived and studied in Europe for some 20 years, then returned to live out her years in Carmel, California, where she died in 1941 at the age of 86.

2
MONTEREY

THE NARROW-GAUGE

railroad track took a sharp curve that routed the train around the end of the sheltering line of hills. Brilliant blue sea flecked with whitecaps and the sudden fresh slap of salt breeze told RLS that his journey was finally almost at an end.

Monterey, once capital of Mexican California, was now a small, pleasant town of some 350 souls, many of them with Spanish or Mexican blood. Most of the buildings were adobe – locally made mud and straw bricks, whitewashed when they had become walls, and topped with red tile or, in some cases, a wooden roof. The walls were thick and retained the heat from inside hearths or kept cool in the heat of summer when properly aired and sheltered by vines and overhanging boughs.

For nearly a month RLS had made a painful and laborious way to what, to a sickly Scotsman who was as yet unsuccessful in his chosen career as a writer, must have seemed a highly unlikely destination. Yet Monterey was the town where Fanny Osbourne was temporarily living, and RLS had already vowed to himself that he was going to marry this woman, 10 years older than he and already with a husband and two children. One thing was in his favor: Fanny had written him that she was in Monterey because she could no longer tolerate her husband's blatant infidelities.

The sight of what he knew must be the Monterey seashore perked him up. The few people with him on the train from Salinas, where the Southern Pacific had deposited him after his boarding at San Francisco, probably couldn't tell the difference in his spirits by looking at him. His diseased lungs had in the past weeks caused him to vomit blood and endure endless coughing spasms. Gaunt by nature, the description most people now used for him was that of scarecrow. He had skimped on food to save money – something that in the long run is always false economy. And on the steamship voyage across the Atlantic he had picked up an ugly case of eczema that covered his hands.

The fact that he was in Monterey was confirmed by a man seated near him at the same moment the train came to a jolting halt. RLS could find nothing in sight that indicated he was near a town. All he could see was sand and an occasional scrubby bush. There was no train station. He was greeted by the same sight found by all arrivals at this abrupt end-of-the-line, including Belle, Fanny's daughter, who years later recalled of her own arrival in Monterey: "The train stopped some distance from Monterey; there was no depot, no platform, only a dusty road. Here several carriages were waiting and a group of horsemen who shouted to our few fellow-passengers in voluble Spanish."

One such carriage – Anne B. Fisher described it in her novelized story of RLS's time in Monterey as "a crossbreed between a drayman's cart and a buggy" – was available for hire. It was driven by one Manuel Wolter, whose descendants are still prominent citizens of the area today. RLS signaled that he needed a ride into town.

The distance was less than a mile. Over the next dune he caught sight of Monterey itself, a rather tidy sprawl of one- and two-story adobes that climbed partway up a hillside crowned with pines. The road followed close to the edge of Monterey Bay for a while, then the bay curved around northward to a point dominated by the Customs House. Manuel Wolter followed the ruts straight toward the hillside, paralleling more or less what is Del Monte Avenue today.

RLS asked as discreetly as he could the whereabouts of Mrs. Osbourne. His driver was able to tell him the Osbournes were staying at rented quarters in Señora Bonifacio's home. They then arrived at the intersection with Monterey's main thoroughfare, Alvarado Street. On the corner—approximately where the Monterey Convention Center and the Doubletree Inn are now located—was the Bohemia Saloon. The proprietors were, a sign proclaimed, the Sanchez Brothers.

Manuel Wolter may have been a mindreader or he may have merely been following instinct; some have written that his horse automatically came to a stop every time he reached the Bohemia Saloon. At any rate, RLS was relieved that he had a few moments to think things over before knocking on Fanny's door.

Sr. Wolter introduced his lone passenger to the few people already bellied up to the bar, and they were immediately intrigued by the stranger's deep voice and Scottish accent, an accent RLS cherished and cultivated as a continuing link to his beloved, if dank, homeland. And within moments he learned of a coincidence: One of the Sanchez brothers, Adolfo, was courting Nellie Van de Grift—Fanny's younger sister!

(For some reason, Belle has always spelled Adolfo's name "Adulfo," and other biographers, such as Rice, have imitated her. She also spelled the name of their landlady in Monterey, Maria Ygnacia Bonifacio—known by the nickname for Ygnacia, Nachita—as Señora

ALVARADO STREET, MONTEREY'S MAIN THOROUGHFARE,
AT THE TIME OF RLS'S RESIDENCE THERE.

Bonifascio. Neither of these spellings is either Spanish or correct, and it is a mystery why the usually precise Belle did this.)

RLS planked down the necessary silver for a searing shot of brandy, retiring to the side of the good-natured company there assembled so he could gather his thoughts. It was not considered good manners to mention a proper lady's name in a saloon, much less to ask questions about her. The country-bred Manuel Wolter, however, apparently had few compunctions, and it was from his steady commentary that RLS learned the answers to his most burning questions: (1) How did this throng happen to know so much about the Van de Grift-Osbournes? (2) Was Sam Osbourne in town? The answer to the first question was, of course, the well-known courtship by Adolfo of Nellie; the answer to the second question was, to an obviously relieved RLS, no. He was back in Oakland and, as Fanny soon told him, with another of his "ladies."

This was Saturday, August 30, 1879, and RLS must have noted it was close to 5 in the afternoon. It had been nearly three months since Fanny's letter had reached him in Scotland. He himself had been ill with what has been described as neuralgia. He had gone to Paris to recuperate in the change of climate. In the meantime he had sent off what money he could to Fanny to augment the funds allowed her by her erratic husband. He had sent her £20 by way of her brother, Jacob, who was living in Riverside, California, at the time, and later as much as £50 in care of Joe Strong in Pacific Grove. In those days a pound was worth $5 American and had the buying power of something like $50 at today's value. RLS was able to buy a full meal in both Monterey and San Francisco for 50¢!

RLS had an allowance of £250 a year from his parents at this time, plus extras as needed for trips to the Continent and care for his health. He was not yet famous as a writer, but he was published and he was getting underway. He was getting as little as £5 for a story, but more usually between £20 and £50 for his work when it appeared in print. In 1874, he had had his first three articles published in English literary magazines, an event that had made things easier at home for him because his father saw that, although his only son would never build a lighthouse, nor would he even argue a case in court, his writing was worthy of publication. His allowance was increased. His earlier work appeared in the magazine *Cornhill*, whose editor was Leslie Stephen, father of Virginia Woolf. *Cornhill* magazine did not pay the top prices of the day, but it helped establish him among the members of the literary world who counted, especially the editors, the critics . . . and his circle of friends.

Then the years when he had first known—and, it is reported, made love to—Fanny he had two books published. The first was *An Inland Voyage*, which described his canoe trip in France with such friends as Sir Walter Simpson, 1878. The next year *Travels With a Donkey*, recounting his famous trek in France's Cevennes with Modestine, was published. Both were well received critically but failed to produce a public rush to the bookstores.

Then, even though he had failed to win a commission as a roving correspondent for the *Times of London* to finance his voyage as he had hoped, he booked passage on the ship *Devonia* for New York. Much has been made of RLS's poverty at this time of his life, but in fact he always had money available to him, and his not going First Cabin was his own choice: "I was not, in truth, a steerage passenger," he wrote in his book *The Amateur Emigrant*. "Although anxious to see the worst of emigrant life, I had some work to finish on the voyage, and was advised to go by the second cabin, where at least I should have a table at command." And so he boarded the *Devonia* on the River Clyde at Greenock and . . . "We steamed out of the Clyde on Thursday night." It was August 7, 1879.

He arrived in New York August 17, somewhat worse for the wear. He immediately posted back to London the story—his first venture into fiction—which he had managed to complete on board, "The Story of a Lie." New York was in the midst of a rainy season and the fragile RLS felt his lungs deteriorating rapidly. He spent some time, unsuccessfully, calling on editors. On August 19, he took the train ferry from New York to Jersey City, across the Hudson River, and eventually boarded the immigrant train that was to take him West under conditions he described as "downright misery and danger."

Three thousand miles and nearly 12 days later, the ordeal of travel by immigrant train was over. He had his first glimpse of San Francisco Bay. A ferry ride took him to San Francisco's Southern Pacific terminal. And now he must have mused to himself, "Here I am in the American West, and in a Spanish town." Monterey.

RLS had with him a trunk, or sea chest, as some have described it. It would not be delicate for him to arrive at the doorstep of a married woman with such obvious baggage; so he left it with the Sanchez brothers and had Manuel Wolter deliver him to the neat adobe home presided over by Doña Nachita Bonifacio and her mother. The two-story, red tiled home was a block on down Alvarado Street.

RLS and Fanny had corresponded as regularly as they could. When he arrived in New York, he had picked up a letter from her at general delivery. His arrival was therefore not unexpected.

Fanny's son Lloyd was then 12. Years later, in 1924, he was to write a book for Charles Scribner's Sons called *An Intimate Portrait of R.L.S.* in which he recalled:

It was here one morning in our sitting room that my mother looked down at me rather oddly, and, with a curious brightness in her eyes, said: "I have news for you. Luly's coming." I think RLS must have arrived the next day. I remember his walking into the room, and the outcry of delight that greeted him; the incoherence, the laughter, the tears; the heart-welling joy of reunion. Until that moment I had never thought of him as being in ill health. On the contrary, in vigor and vitality he had always seemed among the foremost of those young men at Grèz; and though he did not excel in any of the sports, he had shared in them exuberantly. Now he looked ill, even to my childish gaze; the brilliancy of his eyes emphasized the thinness and palor of his face. His clothes no longer picturesque but merely shabby, hung loosely on his shrunken body; and there was about him an indescribable lessening of his alertness and self-confidence.

For a boy of 12, Lloyd had an unusually keen eye. Of course, some of his childhood memories would have been reinforced by constant retelling over the years; and all of us have "memories" that are at least half inspired by our elders who have so often told us, "You remember the day when. . . ."

Yet of all those who made up the family RLS was soon to marry into, only Lloyd was to become a successful writing partner with RLS. Fanny wanted desperately to be considered as creative as her husband—and in her own way she was—but her brilliance never crossed over the borderline to genius, and that of RLS did. Fanny tried at least twice to collaborate in writing with her husband, and both attempts have been critically adjudged failures. One was a play, *The Hanging Judge,* which they wrote together in 1887; RLS's editor in London read it and hid it away in embarrassment. The other instance was *More New Arabian Nights—The Dynamiter.* It, too, is considered inferior among the works to bear the Robert Louis

Stevenson name. Fanny is said to have written *The Dynamiter* by herself in 1884.

RLS was, indeed, about to marry into a most remarkable family. Both Fanny and Belle were unusually talented individuals, and they are important people in their own right. This will be borne out again and again as the RLS drama unfolds. Lloyd did become a successful collaborator with RLS, and Belle's son, Austin, was destined to become an acclaimed playwright.

Young Lloyd probably did have very vivid memories of his beloved "Luly" that he was able to recall on his own and to record in later years. Following the foregoing passage in his 1924 book, Lloyd added: "This fleeting impression passed away as I grew more familiar with him in our new surroundings. Certainly he had never seemed gayer or more light-hearted, and he radiated laughter and good spirits. His talk was all about the people he was meeting, and he gave me my first understanding of the interest to be derived from human nature . . ."

Joe Strong was very much in evidence all this time, and although Fanny may have had it in the back of her mind that an artist was not a suitable match for her daughter, she may also have had some thoughts about the fact that she was in love with an apparently penniless writer.

At this point, RLS's first day in Monterey, what he needed most was a place to stay. Joe took him to a rooming house run by Rosanna Leese, whose family, headed by David Leese, ran a saloon located in those days at the corner of Pearl and Tyler streets in Monterey. The rooming house itself has long since disappeared, but it was located between two buildings still standing on Calle Principal just east of Jefferson Street: the Larkin House, a magnificent adobe now maintained by the California Department of Parks and Recreation, built in 1834 by Thomas Oliver Larkin, a highly successful Yankee merchant who became the U.S. consul to Mexican California in 1843–1847, a building RLS passed daily while on his walks about Monterey; and the so-called Sherman Rose Adobe, so named because legend had it that Lt. William Tecumseh Sherman – later a hero of the Civil War but then a junior officer stationed in Monterey – had wooed Doña Nachita there and had planted a rose on the eve of his departure for new duty to commemorate their love . . . This charming story was dashed by Doña Nachita herself in an interview shortly before her death in which she stated she had no idea how the tale started and she really did not remember meeting Lt. Sherman at all.

Mrs. Leese was suspicious of the frail stranger with the odd accent, but she admitted him to a sparsely furnished sleeping room after he had paid $7 in advance for the week.

At the end of that week, she refused to keep him on. She had taken note of the eczema which, from all reports, presented a revolting sight to all except those who loved him. After he departed, she burned the bedding he had used.

3
C̲ARMEL̲
V̲ALLEY̲

T̲HE SIGN ON THE SMALL

structure on Calle Principal, beside the gardens of the Larkin House, implies that the building is the Sherman Rose Adobe. The original Sherman Rose Adobe, of course, was the home of Nachita Bonifacio, where Fanny Osbourne and her family were staying in the fall of 1879. When RLS knew this house, it was located in downtown Monterey on Alvarado Street where a newer, two-block street begins. This little street is called Bonifacio Place.

After RLS and the Osbournes were long gone, the fine old adobe was moved, brick by brick, up a hillside not quite a mile away. It is still there today on Mesa Road, an elite residential area, and the famed bower of roses continues to flourish. It is marked by a sign proclaiming it the Casa Bonifacio, but it is a private residence and not open to the public.

Young Lloyd remembers the house in these terms: "Our home was a small, two-storied, rose-embowered adobe cottage fronting on Alvarado Street; my mother rented it from two old Spanish ladies named Bonifacio, who lived in an upper part of it in a seclusion comparable to that of the Man with the Iron Mask. The only time they ever betrayed their existence was when the elder would scream at me in Spanish from an upper window to leave the calf alone. Our back yard pastured this promising young animal, and it was an inspiriting pastime to lasso it, especially from the back of my pony when my mother and grown-up sister were absent. But Señora Bonifacio was never absent, though always slow in coming into action . . ."

This passage is important not only for the childhood memory of the home RLS came to know but also for as yet another key to the personality of Sam Osbourne, the philandering husband, for it was he who had bought Samuel Lloyd, his son, the pony especially for the Monterey stay. Sam also paid the rent, something the 12-year-old boy apparently was not aware of. He only knew that his mother and father had recently decided to remove themselves from Oakland and that the family, then he, his sister, and his Aunt Nellie, had been told they, too, could visit Monterey. At the same time, the boy's father was smiling and generous, but more and more absent.

Many years later Belle was to write in her autobiography:

It shocks me now to remember how little I noticed that my father's visits grew fewer and fewer. At first, he joined us over the week-ends, going back to San Francisco on Sunday nights; then several weeks would pass, and often when he did come, Nellie and I would be sent away while he and my mother held agitated conferences. I know now they were discussing a divorce.

It wasn't until long after that I learned of the indignant letters my mother's brothers and sisters wrote to her. Divorces were very rare then, and considered disgraceful. Her family was appalled at the idea and wrote frantic protests against it.

RLS had arrived in Monterey during one of those prolonged absences of the husband of the woman he fully intended to marry. After the initial hesitancy of that first day, when he wondered what the citizenry would think of Fanny Osbourne because a sickly foreign bachelor had come 6,000 miles across an ocean and a continent to be with her, he found himself welcomed almost as a member of the family. And although it was Fanny's letter that had brought him to Monterey, it was at this point Lloyd, Belle, and Nellie—and, yes, even Joe Strong—who made him feel so welcome at Casa Bonifacio.

It is a little difficult now to think of Alvarado Street as a place of homes as well as of businesses. As the passage by Lloyd tells us, Casa Bonifacio then fronted on Alvarado, the commercial street, while the backyard was quite rural. Today the backyard is Tyler Street, which has been commercial for so long now that it is run down, partly torn down, and on the way toward commercial renewal. Where Lloyd irritated Doña Nachita's mother by lassoing a calf, there is now a parking lot shared by a bank and a music store!

"My father had rented an entire wing of this roomy old adobe house set in the midst of a walled garden full of flowers and fruit trees," Belle wrote of their summer home in Monterey. And she gave this description of the inside of Casa Bonifacio: "Nellie and I slept in an upstairs room overlooking the garden. It was a noble room, its walls three feet thick, and the ceiling beams hand carved. We hung our dresses and starched white petticoats in a large wardrobe with carved doors. There was a marble-topped washstand with pitcher and basin, and a huge bed with a canopy, and we kept our underclothes and fripperies in a lovely old painted chest. I suppose there were chairs, but I don't remember any. On a commode beside the bed, we always kept a candle and matches, for the charming Spanish custom of the serenade still prevailed, and the only response expected was to show a light."

It was for Nellie's sake that the candle and matches were ever at the ready. And RLS met the reason for all this within his first hour in Monterey. Explained Belle: "There were no class distinctions in Monterey; we danced with the butcher, the baker, and – the saloon keeper. Particularly with the saloon keeper, for Adulfo {sic} Sanchez was the most popular young man in Monterey. He belonged to one of the oldest families there, his father and grandfather having once owned half the county. He was young, extraordinarily handsome, and was gifted with a glorious baritone voice. And he fell deeply in love with Nellie." The baritone voice was heard often beneath that second-story window at Casa Bonifacio.

Belle also has left us a description of the Monterey that she and RLS knew: "I had known vaguely that California had once belonged to Spain, and then to Mexico, but I was not at all prepared to find Monterey so foreign. I could hardly believe I was in the United States. As we drove down the main street, we exclaimed at the old adobe buildings with their iron balconies and red tile roofs. The narrow sidewalks were mostly of wooden planks, but here and there we saw some made of the vertebras of whales. At the street corners old Spanish cannons were stuck upright to serve as hitching posts.

Occasionally, through the open doorways, we caught glimpses of patios, gay with potted plants, and the entrance to one garden was under an arch contrived of the curving jaw bones of a whale."

Whaling, of course, was still a business off the Monterey coast during the time of RLS. One of the first people RLS met in Monterey was a sheriff's deputy for that area, Mike Noon, who was also a whaler. The Monterey coast is today populated with the descendants of Portuguese whalers who came to California because of their expertise, gained in the Azores, in whaling. Today Portuguese and Spanish names are often confused by those not acquainted with the difference between these Iberian neighbors. And Mike Noon's daughter, the late Flora Noon, once told me her father personally killed the last whale taken in Monterey Bay, in 1901, as I recall her saying. He did not go to sea, as some of the Portuguese did, but rather manned a land station from which a stray whale would be waylaid. Fortunately, petroleum was becoming more and more available, ending the need for whale oil for illumination, and the Portuguese took up cattle ranching, providing tastier steaks than did the hapless cetaceans.

During these first days in Monterey, RLS was attempting to regain some of the health he had lost on the arduous voyage both aboard the *Devonia* across the Atlantic and on the immigrant train across America. He allowed himself only 50¢ a day for meals, but there is much evidence that he usually had a free second meal with Fanny Osbourne at Casa Bonifacio. At the same time, Fanny was going through an agonizing search of her soul about the probability of divorce. She knew she could never count on her husband to be faithful exclusively to her. It not only wasn't his nature, but he was still a dashing appearing man, more youthful than she in looks, blond, with a rakish beard, and an admirer of good restaurants and dancing. He seems never to have lacked a partner.

On the other hand, divorce was such a shocking thing in those days she could count on complete ostracism from her parents' family. She also wondered what effect it would have on her son, Lloyd, her daughter, Belle, and even her sister, Nellie. She need not have worried about Nellie, who was as liberated a female as was Fanny. And she need not have worried about young Lloyd, who had seen his father only during brief visits for most of his life. Only Belle held reservations and, as we have seen, many years later she regretted them.

But during that first week in Monterey, RLS sensed that Fanny was holding back. He wondered if she were having second thoughts about the letter she had written that brought him to Monterey. On top of that, the Monterey fog was about to do what the Atlantic and the overland railroad trip had started: It was about to finish him off.

As Belle recorded, love was all about RLS: ". . . the quiet studious Nellie, rather prim, and given to serious reading, became very fond of Adulfo. Joe Strong devoted himself to me, and with Ninole (Joe's sister) and her swain, a young rancher, we formed a merry group. There were riding parties to Point Lobos, picnics on the beach, swimming off the wharf, and gay weekly fandangos where we soon learned the old Spanish dances."

Gregarious Joe Strong had come to know just about everyone in old Monterey and the surrounding countryside. One of the people to whom he introduced RLS was a young Englishman named Edward Berwick, who had obtained property in Carmel Valley, which he farmed and on which he raised a small number of cattle. Although RLS was pleased to hear the English accents again, he made certain to emphasize his own Scottishness in his conversations with him. Berwick lived until 1934 and late in life recorded some reminiscences of his meetings with RLS, although they apparently became slightly fogged with the passage of time. He claims to have had RLS and Joe Strong at his place on at least two occasions. It now appears that RLS accompanied Joe there once, but the second time RLS was strictly on his own.

RLS was dispirited. After coming what, to him, was halfway across the world to see the woman he loved, he found her still unprepared to take that final step and ask for a divorce. He realized his health was at a dangerous level. The summer fogs so famous in the Monterey area had not yet ended, and they tortured his fragile lungs. Then Fanny got word that Sam was coming down for a weekend visit. One writer, Anne B. Fisher, says RLS himself picked up the letter at the post office and carried it to Fanny; scholars such as Roger S. Swearingen think this unlikely. However the news arrived, between the impending arrival of Fanny's husband and the state of his health, he decided to leave Monterey for a few days and take a camping trip high up in the mountains. Most of all he wanted to leave the fog behind and ease the constant pain in his lungs. Some accounts say RLS left Monterey because Fanny had temporarily departed for Oakland. The impending visit of her husband, however, makes more sense. And Mr. Berwick, in his recollections, does say that RLS told him he left Monterey because Fanny was gone, and he wanted to save on rent money.

Whatever the reason, the most certain is his health. He rented a spring wagon and two horses from Manuel Wolter and started over the hill to the mouth of Carmel Valley. It would make sense that he paused briefly on the lower side of the hill to look at the ruins of the Carmel Mission, Misión San Carlos de Borromeo, where the saintly Fr. Junipero Serra lay buried in the nearly roofless church he had called "the jewel of the California missions."

Then he turned east into the long valley and allowed his horses to take their own time for some two miles. Here he arrived at the Berwick Ranch. The last remains of this place vanished before the developers' bulldozer in the mid-1970s, when the famous Berwick barn came down. It endured from the time of RLS for some ninety years, and somehow always looked old. Shingles were often missing from the roof, and its beams developed a dignified sag in old age. While it stood, it was probably one of the most sketched buildings in the area, not only because of its character, but because of its association with RLS.

The lovesick, hacking, confused Scotsman arrived at the Berwick Ranch perhaps an hour or so before sundown. The Englishman was busy with his chores, but put them aside, called to his wife that there was a visitor, and helped RLS take the harnesses off his horses and prepare them for the night. They discussed California history — RLS was fascinated with the Bancroft volumes and had purchased the set — and Mrs. Berwick brought tea and, later, supper. And when it came time to go to bed, RLS went to the barn and bedded down in the hay. Although Berwick says this is what RLS preferred, the apparent fact of the matter is that Mrs. Berwick was horrified by the eczema on RLS's hands and would not allow him to use one of their spare beds.

The next morning the sun was shining brightly, and although RLS was doubtless still down in the dumps because of his beloved Fanny's apparent vacillation, the warm sunshine did wonders for his ailing lungs and frail frame. Another 4 miles and he reached the entrance to Robinson Canyon — where the Farm Center is located today. There was a passable trail and it was obvious that it climbed quickly up into the Santa Lucia Mountains – the heights RLS sought to escape the fog and gain the clear air for which his lungs cried out.

He had not prepared himself well with provisions; the only thing he mentions ingesting is tea. His horses pulled the light wagon uphill all through the day, making tight turn after turn, disappearing into thick groves of redwoods, those magnificent trees believed to be the oldest on earth, survivors of the Paleolithic Age. Then he would burst out into the open and view a series of round hills where cattle grazed.

At these higher reaches, the land on both sides of him was owned by Bradley Sargent, one of four brothers who had made vast property acquisitions and had acquired considerable wealth and influence. The town of Bradley, down low in the Salinas Valley, was named after this particular brother; he was a state senator at about this time. The ranch was named the San Francisquito (Little St. Francis) and was later combined with another ranch, El Potrero de

THE MONTEREY FOG WHICH RLS SO DREADED SNAKES ITS
WAY INTO THE LOWER REACHES OF THE SAN CARLOS
RANCH, WHERE RLS WAS RESCUED FROM NEAR DEATH.

San Carlos (the Pasture of St. Charles), which is entered from Carmel Valley near the old Berwick Ranch at what is today the beginning of the Carmel Valley Golf and Country Club. Bradley Sargent eventually divested himself of the property, and it was bought around 1911 by a mysterious Englishman of wealth of unknown origins named George Gordon Moore. Moore sold it in 1936 to the present owner's father, Arthur C. Oppenheimer. I lived on the ranch, now called the Rancho San Carlos, for nearly six years; it is one of several coincidences that have brought me close to RLS's spirit.

As night was about to fall, RLS reached the small San Clemente Creek. He had not eaten properly and had not been properly attended by a doctor since the end of his emigrant trip ordeal. RLS records that he recalls getting off his wagon, hitching the horses and fixing a small fire to boil water for tea. But for the next two days he remembers only small incidents as if seen in a fog. Mostly he remembers preparing tea, then passing hours at a time in fever and labored sleep punctuated with devastating nightmares.

4
THE STEVENSON
HOUSE

A FEW DAYS LATER,

RLS wrote to Sir Sidney Colvin, a Cambridge professor who, as much as anyone, discovered RLS as a writer: "Here is another curious start to my life. I am living at an angora goat ranch in the Coast Line Mountains, 18 miles from Monterey. I was camping out, but got so sick that the two Rancheros took me in and tended me. One is an old bear hunter, 72 years old, and a captain from the Mexican war; the other a pilgrim and one who was out with the bear flag and under Fremont when California was taken by the states."

A month later he wrote a letter dated October 8, 1879, to Sir Edmund Gosse, a critic, editor and friend introduced to him in London by Sir Sidney: "I was pretty nearly slain; my spirit lay down & kicked for three days; I was up at an Angora goat ranche in the Santa Lucia Mountains, nursed by an old frontiersman, a mighty hunter of bears, and I scarcely slept or ate or thought for four days. Two nights I lay out under a tree, in a sort of stupor, doing nothing but fetch water for myself & horse —[RLS's reference to "horse" in the singular seems to bear out Mr. Berwick's recollection that he found the two horses RLS had rented from Manuel Wolter unsuited to mountain climbing, and he lent him a more powerful horse of his own and kept the two Wolter horses for him at the Berwick property]—light a fire and make coffee, and all night awake hearing the goat bells ringing and the tree frogs singing when each new noise was enough to set me mad. Then the bear hunter came around, pronounced me 'real sick' and ordered me up to the ranche."

Tradition has it that the bear hunter had to lift RLS up and carry him inside his cottage, so far gone was the ailing Scotsman. The bear hunter was Jonathan Wright, who owned the property together with the other man mentioned, Anson Smith. Adds Swearingen (*Chronology 1879–1880*): "Besides Smith and Wright, there were living at the ranch an Indian servant and three children: Sarah Wright (later Mrs. E.J. Bolce), Dolly Wright (later Mrs. Frank Darling), and a stepsister, Millie Claudie (later Mrs. Birks). Mrs. Wright, as Stevenson noted, was not there at the time, being 'from home sick'. . . . According to (Anne) Fisher, Mrs. Wright 'was lying sick at the Customs House (in Monterey) where her aunt, Mrs. Lambert, lived.'"

Jonathan Wright nursed RLS back to some semblance of health. After two or three days, he regained his voice, but knew better than to force this extra strain on his lungs except when absolutely necessary. He sat up in his bed and outlined his recollections of his days on the immigrant train, later to be part of his book, *The Amateur Emigrant*. RLS said in one of his letters that he taught the Wright children their alphabet, but years later Sarah Wright Bolce said she only remembers that he told them stories.

The staple of this ranch family was goat meat, but RLS couldn't stomach it and they cooked venison for him in a separate cast iron pot. In 1962, this pot was presented to the Stevenson House.

After three weeks in the clear air of the Santa Lucias, RLS was well enough to head back down Robinson Canyon. The remains of the cottage in which he lived are still there to be viewed from the road. I watched over the years as vandals and trespassers hauled away shingles, beams, fireplace stones, anything they could take either as a souvenir of RLS or, more often than not, just to wreak havoc on the innocent building. Since those days, security on the Rancho San Carlos has been considerably tightened up, and the curious who make the 20-minute drive up Robinson Canyon Road from Carmel Valley Road should not climb the fence onto the private property. The cabin's skeleton can be seen clearly enough little more than 100 yards from where the road crosses over the creek.

At the end of the last week of September, RLS returned to Monterey. He went directly to see Fanny. She had already heard how ill he had been. Jonathan Wright had been to town to visit his ailing wife and left behind tales of the Scotsman he had discovered nearly dead by the San Clemente Creek.

Several biographers say that it was at this point Fanny finally realized how much she loved RLS. She had almost lost him and now she determined that she would indeed ask Sam for the divorce.

Meanwhile RLS had to find a place to stay. Mrs. Leese would not have him back. She put it to him politely by saying she would be forced to raise the rent to $10 a week. His budget would not stand that.

Through the old Frenchman, Jules Simoneau, at whose restaurant RLS took his one meal a day, he learned of what would one day become known as the Stevenson House. It was then called the French Hotel. It was in part the private residence of Doña Manuela Girardin, whose daughter was the wife of Dr. J.P. Heintz. Dr. Heintz was the physician RLS consulted, and this apparently accounts for some of the inaccurate reports by biographers that RLS went to live with the doctor himself.

The building was actually two buildings combined into one. The original section was built in the late 1830s and was first lived in by Rafael Gonzales, who was Mexico's first administrator of customs in Alta (Upper) California. His office, of course, remains a brisk three-block walk toward the harbor where the Customs House, the oldest government building west of the Rockies, still stands. Both the Customs House and the Stevenson House are maintained today by the California Department of Parks and Recreation, with guided tours available hourly six days a week. The Stevenson House is located on Houston Street, between Pearl and Webster Streets.

The street side of the Stevenson House is maintained as a Monterey home of the 19th century and contains authentic period furnishings and costumes. The rest is devoted to RLS, for the most part filled with his own furniture. The pieces were bought by the State from Belle during the last years of her life in Santa Barbara. Each piece of furniture has a separate descriptive, authenticating sheet signed by her. We therefore are assured that we are looking at a dining table once owned by RLS and upon which his coffin ultimately rested after he died in Samoa. There is a small table on which it is known he did his writing when at sea on one of his chartered yachts.

The furnishings in the room RLS occupied were not there when he was, but they belonged to him later. They came from his home, Skerryvore, at Bournemouth, England, where he and Fanny lived for several years after they left California. At the time RLS moved into his second-story room in the French Hotel on Houston Street, most of the transient tenants were seamen. The rooms rented at $2 or $3 a week, depending on how they were furnished. There is some confusion as to how RLS's room was furnished. It appears to me that it may not have been furnished at all. He did write glowing letters to his concerned parents in Scotland and his literary friends in London describing ". . . great airy rooms with five windows opening on a balcony." This is obviously an attempt to allay any fears that he was suffering, for the Stevenson House has no balconies and no room with more than two windows. He apparently slept rolled in a blanket on the bare floor.

THE GIRARDIN RESIDENCE–FRENCH HOTEL,
NOW KNOWN AS THE STEVENSON HOUSE,
WHERE RLS LIVED IN MONTEREY.

It was in Monterey that RLS formed what was to become the most cherished friendship of his life. This was with Jules Simoneau, a Frenchman who was then 58 years old. He ran a small restaurant in a building that has long vanished but that was situated on what is called today Jules Simoneau Plaza. (The local public bus company uses the four sides of this plaza as the base of its operations over the entire Peninsula, Carmel Valley, Big Sur and Salinas. The drivers are in constant touch with home base by radio and refer to the site as Transit Plaza. This infuriates W.I. Eugene, the guide at the Stevenson House. "Every time we approach Simoneau Plaza, the driver yells 'Transit Plaza.' I make a point of getting off by the front door so I can look the driver in the eye and say, 'This is Simoneau Plaza!'")

The many references to old Jules Simoneau by the 29-year-old Scotsman make it plain that RLS not only held the Frenchman in high regard, but considered his daily meal at his restaurant a valuable human experience. Young Lloyd, in his admiration for "Luly," perhaps saw things differently. "I was old enough to appreciate how poor he was," Lloyd wrote in his book years later, "and it tore at my boyish heart that he should take his meals at a grubby little restaurant with men in their shirt-sleeves, and have so bare and miserable a room in the old adobe house . . ."

It appears that Joe Strong, who knew of the place because it was frequented by his fellow artists, introduced RLS to the Simoneau cuisine. Wrote Belle in *This Life I've Loved*: "It was Charles Warren Stoddard, the poet, who really had turned Monterey into an artists' colony. Coming down to see the old [Carmel] Mission, he was so enchanted with the place that he sent word to his friends Joe Strong, Julian Rix and Jules Tavernier. They came to look, and remained to paint. There were endless subjects: fishing boats, whalers, the magnificent breakers dashing against a rocky shore, the amazing Monterey cypress trees, and most popular of all, the Carmel Mission, then a beautiful ruin, undamaged by the loving hands that so dreadfully restored it."

It's unfortunate that Belle could not know the Mission in more recent years. Restoration did, indeed, begin in 1884, in part through efforts that resulted from RLS's urgings in the local newspaper, the *Monterey Californian*. But this early restoration was stopgap work at best. Many years later expert restoration was undertaken under the guidance of the late Sir Harry Downie – knighted by Pope Pius

XII for his restoration work at a number of the California missions –
and even the critical Belle would have approved.

Nellie, who at this time announced her engagement to Adolfo
Sanchez, recalls that RLS was not restricted to a single meal a day, but
often ate with Fanny and her brood, in addition to the meal at
Simoneau's:

. . . The two-story dwelling of the Señorita Maria Ygnacia Bonifacio . . .
we had our temporary residence, and here he {RLS} came often to visit us
and share our simple meals, each of which became a little fete in the thrill
of his presence and conversation. Something he had in him that made life
seem a more exciting thing, better worth living, to everyone associated
with him, and it seemed impossible to be dull or bored in his company. It is
true that he loved to talk, and one of his friends complained that he was
"too deuced explanatory," but it seemed to me that flood of talk he sometimes poured out was the overflow of a full mind, a mind so rich in ideas
that he could well afford to bestow some of it upon his friends without
hope of return.

His was no narrow vein to be jealously hoarded for use in his writings, but his difficulty lay rather in choosing from the wealth of his store.
He has remarked that he could not understand a man's having to struggle
to find "something to write about," and perhaps it is true that one who has
to do that has no real vocation as a writer. . . .

The unexpected discovery in the town of Jules Simoneau, to whom
he refers in his letters as "a most pleasant old boy, with whom I discuss
the universe and play chess," a man of varied talents, who was able to fur-
nish him with an excellent dinner, as well as the intelligent companion-
ship which he valued more than food, was a great satisfaction to him.
Often we all repaired together to Simoneau's little restaurant, where we
were served meals that were a rare combination of French and Spanish
cookery, for our host's wife, Doña Martina, was a native of Miraflores, in
Lower California, and was well-skilled in the preparation of the *tamales*
and *carne con chile* of the Southwest.

It has always seemed to me that in the oft-told story of the friendship between Jules Simoneau and Robert Louis Stevenson but scant justice has been done to the uncommonly fine woman, Doña Martina, who,
no doubt, had her part in caring for the sick writer when he lay so ill in
Monterey.

As a matter of fact, at one point during RLS's stay in Monterey,
Simoneau noted that his friend had not appeared to eat for three
days in a row. He went to the French Hotel, opened the door to RLS's

room after receiving no response to banging on the door, and found RLS on the bare floor, wrapped in a blanket and a cloak, feverish and unable to get up to ask for help. From this instance we gather he did not have a furnished room and we learn one more example of old Jules Simoneau's thoughtfulness.

Dr. Heintz was called, and it was Jules and Doña Martina Simoneau who administered to the ill writer, while Fanny discreetly remained in the background and sent him soups and other foods. She was still very conscious of being a married woman, of being accompanied by a son and daughter by the husband, and quite possibly was not aware of the fact that she was a favorite topic of the local ladies' gossip. By now she knew divorce was her only solution, but she was determined to carry on in as dignified a manner as possible. And there was yet another woman who nursed RLS at this point: the ancient Indian Jacinta, who helped out at Simoneau's restaurant. While RLS lay sick at the French Hotel, she brought him medicine of her own that she rubbed on his hands and cured him of the ugly eczema, which the ointments of Dr. Heintz, the man of medicine from Luxembourg, had failed to do.

Relatively healthy again in a few days, RLS resumed his routine of roaming about on foot on the Monterey Peninsula, visiting Fanny Osbourne, her son, Lloyd, her daughter, Belle—usually accompanied by her suitor, Joe Strong—and Fanny's sister, Nellie, and her suitor, Adolfo. RLS was acutely aware that he appeared to have little to offer his future wife except his love.

If RLS felt anything more keenly that his love for Fanny, it was his calling as a writer. It was for this reason, and this reason alone, that he was so often penniless at this stage of his life. He had money available to him, did make several draws on his London account, and more was available from his parents. He felt strongly, however, that he *must* live on his earnings as a writer if he were to call himself a writer—"a slinger of ink"—honestly. He therefore lived in a rather unhealthy manner as far as adequate accommodations and diet were concerned. This honesty of discipline almost cost him his life.

There were a number of "regulars" who ate their main meal of the day at Simoneau's restaurant, one of them named Crevole Bronson, editor of the *Monterey Californian*. It was Simoneau, the wily old philosopher of Nantes, who understood how important it was to RLS to be both a writer and honest. Simoneau understood RLS's

JULES SIMONEAU, RLS'S FRIEND AND
MENTOR IN MONTEREY.

Robert Louis Stevenson in California

pledge to himself, but the old man wasn't above stretching a point for a good cause. So one day at dinner he told RLS that Bronson had just taken over the *Californian,* that the editor was trying to run the newspaper by himself because he had pretty much spent all his cash reserve to purchase the publication, but that there were many things to write about and perhaps Bronson could afford at least a part-time correspondent.

RLS's eyes must have lit up at the idea. And he was obviously even more elated when he found the editor was anxious to hire him at $2 a week. What RLS didn't know was that at a meal when he had been absent Simoneau got eight of the regular diners to pledge 25¢ a week and also got them and Bronson to pledge their secrecy. This is where the $2 came from. RLS never discovered how he was being surreptitiously helped by the people who had come to admire him as a person.

Lloyd wrote of this:

Conceive my joy . . . when one day he burst in with the news of a splendid job, and prolonged the suspense by making us all try to guess what it was; and my crushing disappointment when it turned out to be as a special reporter on the local paper at two dollars a week.

It was supposed to be a great joke, and I laughed with the rest; but on my part it was a sad and wondering pretense. Two dollars meant eight meals at the fishermen's restaurant. What was to become of poor Luly, who daily looked thinner and shabbier? But afterward my mother reassured me, and I was thrilled to hear of what "experience" meant to a writer, and how in reality Monterey was a kind of gold mine in which Luly was prospering extraordinarily, little though he looked it.

This passage, written by Lloyd as an adult after dredging up the memory from his childhood, is telling for two reasons: In the first place, it tells us of the genuine affection young Lloyd felt toward RLS; and second, it reveals Fanny's true nature and, more important, her real role in the life of her future husband. She was, after all, his most severe, but his most helpful, critic. Young Lloyd was concerned for his friend's health and well-being. Fanny knew that RLS was a genius, a writer the likes of which she could only wish to be. But just as today we often find that our best critics are, themselves, poor performers, Fanny recognized that RLS was only on the threshold of his true calling. She also recognized that his genius had to be encouraged. She was not trying to make her son feel better by telling him that RLS was, in fact, profiting from his apparent misery. She knew he was still doing his spade work in Monterey for a future she was now determined he would have because she would be at his side, not only as critic, but as nurse.

5
THE CARMEL
MISSION

THE *TIMES OF LONDON* WAS

not interested in having RLS as a roving correspondent, but now he was "employed" with the *Monterey Californian*. He took his duties very seriously and turned out a number of articles. Unfortunately, in those days a byline was reserved for celebrities, and RLS was not then a celebrity. Only Editor Bronson merited signed articles. Any writer can testify that to be published encourages the writer to greater industry, and RLS did some writing in addition to his newspaper reporting.

It is known that he wrote the draft for *The Amateur Emigrant* while in Monterey. And, Mrs. Masson tells us, ". . . wrote his story, 'The Pavillion on the Links,' afterwards accepted, to his frank amazement – for he called it 'blood and thunder' – by *Cornhill*; he planned his *Prince Otto*; . . . and he wrote a story, 'A Vendetta in the West,' which remained unpublished, as he was not satisfied with it. Eighty-three pages of this last, and about sixty pages of the draft of *The Amateur Emigrant*, were done before the end of the first month in Monterey, October."

Nellie gives us an idea of how he wrote in this description of life at Casa Bonifacio:

To this house he came often of an afternoon to read the results of his morning's work to the assembled family. While we sat in a circle, listening in appreciative silence, he nervously paced the room, reading aloud in his full, sonorous voice – a voice that always seemed remarkable in so frail a man – his face flushed and his manner rather embarrassed, for, far from being overconfident about his work, he always seemed to feel a sort of shy anxiety lest it should not be up to the mark. He invariably gave respectful attention and careful consideration to the criticism of the humblest of his hearers, but in the end clung with Scotch pertinacity to his own opinion if sure of its justice. . . . In this way we heard 'The Pavillion on the Links,' which he wrote while at Monterey and read to us chapter by chapter as they came from his pen.

What he wrote for the *Monterey Californian* is pure conjecture. Without a byline, there is no proof. However, biographer Anne Roller Issler did some detective work in the Monterey City Library and pored over the microfilms of the issues of that newspaper from October to December of 1879, as have I, and this is her conclusion as it appeared in Volume 34, 1965, of the *Pacific Historical Review*:

Editors of California newspapers and other students of Stevenson have speculated on just which articles appearing in the *Monterey Californian* that fall were written by Robert Louis Stevenson. More, I think, than he is usually credited with. The editor of the *Californian* (there was a rival, the *Democrat*) was new that fall, had been indisposed, and announced in his October 7 issue that a new printer was to assist him. He could just as well have said another reporter or even editor! He, Crevole Bronson, carried the title manager, but that meant owner, editor, reporter, and printer. I think it is likely that Stevenson's position at two dollars the week came nearer being that of assistant editor than that of occasional contributor. Going over the microfilm at the public library, I studied all the issues of the paper with which Robert Louis Stevenson could have helped. There are *many* possibilities in the way of brevities and personals . . .

Mrs. Issler then lists 14 articles published between October 7 and December 23 in which she detects RLS's hand. One has been generally accepted for some time as having been written by him because of other references to it, including indirectly by himself. This concerns San Carlos Day, the day once a year when everyone trekked over the hill from Monterey to the ruins of the Carmel Mission and joined the few surviving Indians in celebrating the feast day of that Mission's patron saint. That was published November 11. On

November 18, an editorial appeared urging the restoration of that mission, which its founder, Fr. Junipero Serra, called "the jewel of all the missions." He left a request that he be buried in this, of all the California missions he founded, and he was.

Mrs. Issler noted that the rival newspaper, *The Democrat,* carried a similar editorial that week and mentioned the *Californian's* "contributor," obviously RLS. The *Californian* reproduced the rival's editorial in full:

A contributor of the Monterey Californian, this week, makes a strong appeal to sentiment in favor of the old church in Carmelo Valley. It is rapidly falling to ruin and he puts up a prayer for its restoration and repair. The tradition is that the church was built by Padre Junipero Serra, whose bones it is known lie somewhere beneath the earthen floor, and that the same mould encloses the earthly remains of Spanish and Mexican governors of the Province, as indistinguishable as those of Serra among similar vestiges of nameless dead. Religious and historical associations cluster about the spot, and, considering how small a cost would preserve the church and, maintain its monumental quality, it is strange that it has not been expended. The walls of the building are solid yet, and the repairs required are simply as to the roof, doors and windows. A couple of thousands would suffice.

The *Californian* issue of October 7, 1879, carried this brief among items printed under the page 2 masthead: "The manager of this paper has been considerably under the weather the last week and has not rustled as he would if it had been otherwise. We are under obligations to N.D. Christy, of the Washington Hotel, for kindly assistance. We are expecting relief for the future in the accession of another printer."

The word "printer" was seemingly used at that time as we would use "journalist" today. The editor or reporter was usually involved in the actual printing of the sheets in those days. And right beside this column are two more bearing what are generally accepted as the first two contributions to the newspaper by RLS. One is labeled "The New Railroad to Monterey" and the other, "The Coolies." The latter article, in subtle ways, reveals a very pronounced trait in RLS—a profound sympathy for the underdog. The article, written at Editor Bronson's assignment, starts: "The San Jose Mercury, noted for its intelligent discussion of all subjects, has this to say on the Chinese question: . . ." The article then continues without any quotation marks whatsoever. It is difficult to say, more than 100 years later, whether the entire article is a reprint or whether it is the *Californian's* rewording of the *Mercury* article, with comments here and there by the *Californian's* writer – RLS.

RLS's sympathy for an underdog cause started to show itself when he was a university student. It continued throughout his life. It nearly got him in deep trouble in Samoa during his last years when he took up the cause of a minority chief. In California he wrote sympathetically about the Chinese and especially about the Spanish and the Mexicans, whom he considered the rightful masters of California, and how the Americans had robbed them of their heritage. In this issue of the *Californian,* the article in question includes passages such as "For a time, of course, the new comers (meaning the Chinese) will be welcomed, but before long murmurs will be heard from the white men and women that they are pushed out of employment by their cheaper labor." This is not proof of the RLS touch, but it is one he was capable of.

If researchers such as Mrs. Issler were looking for articles with more obvious links to RLS, there is one candidate she didn't list that I feel must have come from his pen, carried in the November 25 issue:

While doing our level best one day last week to present an acceptable paper to our patrons, a vehicle was drawn up in front of our office door and descended from it Adolfo Sanchez, who immediately unloaded a *staving* thing from the rear of the delivery, rolled it into our habitation with his compliments and suddenly disappeared. An examination proved that there was a vent in it that distilled a white fluid and which after being allowed to stand for a few minutes, changed its color to a beautiful amber. Tasting it we found it very palpable – so much so that we tasted three several times. We had often seen old Gambrinus [the mythical European king credited with inventing beer] before and had admired him, but we did not propose that the jolly old gentleman should make us despise him the following day so contented ourselves with shaking his hand familiarly with a promise to see him on the morrow. The beer was from the brewery of Lurz *&* Menke of Salinas, for whom the Messers. Sanchez Bros., of the Bohemia, are agents. No better article is to be found in the State, Gentlemen; our respects.

Although news and commercial notices are routinely mixed indiscriminately in the newspapers of that day, there is no particular reason to believe that a keg of beer would be dropped off for free, just for

---

a plug, unless there were a personal attachment – such as between RLS and Adolfo Sanchez, suitor of Fanny's sister Nellie.

The editions of the *Monterey Californian* carried a number of advertisements on a regular basis, one of which was "Salinas Brewery / Salinas City, Cal. / LURZ & MENK / Proprietors / Adolfo Sanchez, Agent for Monterey." The Sanchez brothers themselves ran a simple announcement: "Bohemia Saloon, Sanchez Brothers proprietors, Alvarado Street." And in the edition I Xeroxed from the microfilm of the November 25, 1879, issue: "J. SIMONEAU, / FRENCH RESTAURANT! / Lyon's Ale Depot, / Pearl Street, Monterey / The Best of Liquors & Cigars / Meals at all hours. Good cheer and a good reception."

RLS would be the first to endorse that statement about "good cheer and a good reception." How good, he apparently never learned, for Simoneau and his friends, including Editor Bronson, kept their charade to themselves. And it must be understood that Bronson himself appreciated the help he received in this manner. The RLS touch was never acknowledged by name, but the prominent use of his writings made it obvious they were on the mark.

Interpreters of RLS's life have assigned various kinds of importance to the stories he produced for the *Californian*. Two articles under the title of "Hidden Treasure" are thought to have planted a seed for *Treasure Island*. "The Coolies" obviously inspired future writings pleading the cause of the underdog. Perhaps the most tangible effort one can see daily in the Monterey Peninsula area now is the restored Carmel Mission Basilica. RLS pretty much covered the entire peninsula on foot, all the way down to Point Lobos and out into Carmel Valley. In Nellie's *Scribner's Magazine* article she wrote:

Perhaps nothing about the place interested him more deeply than the old mission of San Carlos Borromeo. . . . Once a year, on San Carlos Day, November 4, the entire population, Catholic and Protestant, young and old, dropped all other occupation and travelled, some on horseback, some in wagons, and a goodly number on foot, over the four miles of dusty road out to the mission which, having been founded in 1770, six years earlier than our Declaration of Independence, may lay claim to a respectable antiquity, as such things go in the New World. At the time of Mr. Stevenson's visit to Monterey the church was fast falling into ruin, and presented a picturesque but melancholy spectacle of decay. Nothing of the roof remained except a few rafters, from which hung bits of the leather thongs by which they had been bound together, for no nails were used in its construction. Within its ruined walls mass was celebrated once a year in honor of its patron, Saint Charles Borromeo, and after the religious services were over all the people joined in a joyous *merienda* (lunch) under the trees, during which vast quantities of *tamales, enchiladas,* and other distinctive Spanish-American viands were generously distributed to friend and stranger, Catholic and Protestant. Mr. Stevenson attended one of these celebrations, and was greatly moved by the sight of the pitiful remnant of aged Indians, sole survivors of Father Serra's once numerous flock, who lifted their quavering voices in the mass.

RLS described the scene himself in "The Old Pacific Capital," which first appeared in *Fraser's Magazine* in London and was later included in the work, "Across the Plains," which has been published separately and as part of *The Amateur Emigrant*":

Only one day in the year, the day before our Guy Fawkes, the padre drives over the hill from Monterey; the little sacristy, which is the only covered portion of the church, is filled with seats and decorated for the

THE CARMEL MISSION AS RLS SAW IT, FIVE YEARS
BEFORE RESTORATION BEGAN.

CARMEL MISSION AS IT APPEARS TODAY, RESTORED
AS FATHER SERRA KNEW IT.

service; the Indians troop together, their bright dresses contrasting with their dark and melancholy faces; and there, among a crowd of somewhat unsympathetic holiday makers, you may hear God served with perhaps more touching circumstances than in any other temple under heaven. An Indian, stone blind and about eighty years of age, conducts the singing; other Indians compose the choir; yet they have the Gregorian music at their finger ends, and pronounce the Latin so correctly that I could follow the meaning as they sang. The pronunciation was odd and nasal, the singing hurried and staccato. "In saecula saeculo-ho-horum," they went, with a vigorous aspirate to every additional syllable. I have never seen faces more vividly lit up with joy than the faces of these Indian singers. It was to them not only the worship of God, nor an act by which they re-called and commemorated better days, but was besides an exercise of cul-ture, where all they knew of art and letters was united and expressed. And it made a man's heart sorry for the good fathers of yore, who had taught them to dig and to reap, to read and to sing, who had given them European mass-books which they still preserve and study in their cot-tages, and who had now passed away from all authority and influence in that land – to be succeeded by greedy land thieves and sacrilegious pistol-shots. So ugly a thing our Anglo-Saxon Protestantism may appear beside the doings of the Society of Jesus.

And in the *Monterey Californian* of November 11, 1879, RLS ended the article he signed "The Monterey Barbarian" with this:

A fine old church, a fine old race, both brutally neglected; a survival, a memory and a ruin. The United States Mint can coin many million more dollars pieces, but not make a single Indian; and when Carmel Church is in the dust, not all the wealth of all the States and Territories can replace what has been lost. No man's word can move the Indians from the ruin that awaits them; but the church? How, my dear Bronson, if you and I put together our little mites and, through the columns of your paper, sought upon all hands to interest others in this useful work of protection? I feel sure that the money would be forthcoming before long; and the future little ones of Monterey would clap their hands to see the old Church, and learn by the sight of it more history than even Mr. Graves and all his successors can manage to teach them out of history books.

6
ADIOS TO
MONTEREY

"BEACHCOMBER," MONTEREY

dubbed him. And, indeed, he often walked the beach for miles, starting at the bay and trending north-northwest. He noticed the sea birds and the "strange sea-tangles new to the European eye." Passing Chinatown, he stopped at the Christian Seaside Resort and met the Reverend A.C. McDougall, a Scot and a Methodist, who in summer preached to thousands under the trees of the campground. Now the Pacific boomed louder. He was approaching the wild angle of the shore where the lighthouse stood. How often he had gone with his father to visit lighthouses! He must stop in and meet the keeper, Allen Luce, a highly literate forty-niner from Martha's Vineyard. One day he did stop and found the keeper playing the piano.

So Mrs. Issler wrote of a day in the life of RLS as he searched for background with which to fill out his stories, as well as waited for the day when Mrs. Osbourne would be free to marry him. Long ago it had seemed to him the proprieties of convention had been sufficiently served and further delay could only be procrastination.

The November 25 edition of the *Monterey Californian* carried this brief item, which must have been penned by RLS: "Joe Strong, the artist, has gone off and done it. He was married in San Francisco Monday, November 17th."

Joe, of course, married Belle, and here's how she tells it in *This Life I've Loved*:

About this time my mother threw a bombshell into our camp by telling Joe she was arranging a very good marriage for me. I had reason to believe the man she had in mind was the tall Kentuckian, for later I sat next to a Southerner at a dinner party who reproached me for jilting his friend. Joe was very much upset by this news and hurried to San Francisco for a talk with my father. On his way back he stopped at Salinas and got a marriage license.

Taking me for a walk on the beach he told me he had my father's consent. Then he begged me to marry him at once without telling anybody. We could go to the cottage in East Oakland, get any clothes I needed and then we'd find rooms in San Francisco, where there was much work waiting for him. And I could do illustrating for a weekly paper. It all sounded delightful.

We climbed over the rocks hand in hand till we came to the "Pacific Grove Retreat." Here Joe led me to a cottage where a minister and his wife were waiting, and almost before I realized what was happening, we were married. . . . Returning to Monterey we boarded the narrow-gauge train, arriving at the cottage in East Oakland without so much as a toothbrush.

Needless to say, Fanny was furious. Both she and Nellie took the train to San Francisco the next day and confronted the newlyweds, but apparently was resigned to the course of events. Writes Elsie Noble Caldwell: "[Belle] did not know then that only Louis saved a frantic mother from hurrying to the metropolis to retrieve an impulsive daughter." The meeting was emotional, but Fanny made no attempt to bring a halt to things. Mostly, she checked things out. "They were too close for any hint of family rupture," Mrs. Caldwell commented. And Belle once again had reason to be grateful to RLS, whom, at this point, she still felt unworthy of her mother's hand.

Sam Osbourne found the Strongs an apartment in San Francisco at an address then known as No. 7 New Montgomery Avenue. "Two enormous rooms with high ceilings connected by folding doors, and across the hall a tiny bathroom and kitchenette," Belle wrote. Joe resumed his career as a successful portraitist, but within months he accepted a commission that, unknown to all parties concerned at that time, would dovetail nicely into the future of Louis and Fanny Stevenson. Sugar baron Claus Spreckels saw Joe's art, liked it, and sent the couple off to Honolulu on commission for works for the company's holdings in the Hawaiian Islands.

When Sam was not making one of his increasingly infrequent weekend visits to Monterey to see his family, RLS filled, in an unspoken manner, the male void in the Osbourne household. As Belle and Fanny have both told us, he probably took a meal a day with Fanny, Lloyd (at this time still called Sam, but only months away from switching to his middle name, Lloyd), Belle, Nellie and their escorts. Young Lloyd especially seemed to feel a particular fondness for him, which as yet escaped his older sister; after all, he had probably gathered more happy memories of his times with RLS than with his father. He was old enough to recognize his father when he came to Grèz, but this was a brief occasion during which his little brother died and was buried in a pauper's yard in Paris. But the summer months in France with RLS were happy, exploratory occasions during which time RLS treated the youth as a partner, not a child. At East Oakland his father had not been a member of the household. In Monterey he was an overnight guest, but he and RLS got to know the shoreline walks described by Mrs. Issler. With RLS, Lloyd got to know Chinatown, since then burned in a single, furious conflagration and now the site of the Hopkins Marine Station, and the Summer Retreat, today's Pacific Grove, whose original neighborhoods have such small building lots because they were drawn up for tents, not permanent wooden homes, which occupy them now. Lloyd visited the lighthouse, too, the very lighthouse that is still there and in operation — now unmanned because of the mechanical age.

RLS had time to make numerous observations, many of them unflattering as to the way the Americans treated the Mexican-American people and their customs. He rightfully pointed out in *The Old Pacific Capital* that this was New Spain first, and the Americans were merely interloping adventurers here:

In a place so exclusively Mexican as Monterey, you saw not only Mexican saddles but true Vaquero riding — men always at the hand-gallop up hill and down dale, and around the sharpest corner. . . . The type of face and character of bearing is surprisingly un-American. The first ranged

from something like pure Spanish, to something, in its sad fixity, not unlike the pure Indian, although I do not suppose there was one of pure
blood of either race in all the country. As for the second, it was a matter of
perpetual surprise to find, in that world of absolutely mannerless Americans, a people full of deportment, solemnly courteous, and doing all this
with grace and decorum. In dress they ran to color and bright sashes. Not
even the most Americanized could always resist the temptation to stick a
red rose in his hat-band. Not even the most Americanized would con-
descend to wear the vile dress hat of civilization.

Spanish was the language of the streets. It was difficult to get along
without a word or two of that language for an occasion. The only com-
munications in which the population joined were with view to amusement. A weekly public ball took place with great etiquette, in addition to
the numerous fandangoes in private houses . . .

Nellie wrote of these weekly dances: "It is true that at the cascarone
balls, at which the entire population, irrespective of age or worldly
position, dressed in silks or in flannel shirts, as the case might be, still
gathered almost weekly in truly democratic comradeship. The egg-
shells were no longer filled with gold dust, as sometimes happened in
the prodigal Spanish days, yet time was still regarded as a thing of so
little value that no one thought of abandoning the pleasures of the
dance until broad daylight."

The *cascarón* is an empty egg filled again with confetti. Monterey holds its Cascarón Ball once a year now, in a building that was
very familiar to RLS and one in which he probably watched the pred-
ecessor of today's annual event – the House of the Four Winds (Casa
de los Cuatro Vientos) on Calle Principal, in the same block as the
Larkin House. In a small community such as Monterey was then,
one or two dance halls were all that could be supported. One popular location was called City Hall and, according to Mrs. Fisher, belonged to the Wolter family. It was located at the corner of Franklin
and Alvarado Streets. In acknowledgments in her book, Mrs. Fisher
writes: "For details of this dance and others given that winter, I am
indebted to Mrs. Salisbury Field and to Mrs. M.M. Gragg (née
Hattie Sargent, who gave the dance) and also to Mrs. Locan (née
Ninole Strong), who was the sister of Joe Strong."

My former editor at the *Monterey Peninsula Herald*, James
Gragg Costello, grandson of Hattie Sargent Gragg, told me members
of his family recall seeing the Strongs at several of the dances in those

days, but they do not specifically recall seeing RLS. RLS probably would not have gone openly to a dance as Fanny's escort because of the convention of those days, but it appears he did attend some one way or another. Hattie Sargent was the daughter of Bradley Sargent, who at that time owned what is today the Rancho San Carlos and was soon to acquire title to the old goat ranch where RLS spent three weeks recovering from one of his close calls with death. Jimmie Costello recalls spending summer days at that very cottage, which helps lay to rest stories that the structure we see today is the remains of one built subsequent to RLS's stay there.

If the near loss of RLS to death in the upper reaches of the San Carlos Ranch had cinched Fanny's resolve to marry her Scottish writer, the elopement of her daughter is probably the event that prodded her into action.

Several biographers have written accounts of what happened next, many of which appear to be based on young Lloyd's memory of what happened. The accounts coincide perfectly with those RLS left behind. Wrote Lloyd in later years of that final visit to Monterey by his father, Sam Osbourne:

I had looked forward eagerly to his visit, and it was disconcerting to find him so preoccupied and with so little time to devote to me. He seemed forever to be talking with my mother in a seclusion I was not allowed to disturb. Once as I was studying my lessons in an adjoining room and felt that strangely disturbing quality in their subdued voices—reproaches on her side and a most affecting explanation on his of his financial straits at the time of my little brother's death—I suddenly overheard my mother say, with an intensity that went through me like a knife: "Oh, Sam, forgive me!"

I knew nothing of what all this meant until shortly afterward as I was taking a walk with Stevenson. He was silent and absorbed; I might not have been there at all for any attention he paid me. . . .

All at once he spoke, and here again was this strange, new intonation, so colorless and yet so troubling, that had recently affected the speech of all my elders. "I want to tell you of something," he said."You may not like it, but I hope you will. I am going to marry your mother."

I could not have uttered a word to save my life. I was stricken dumb. . . .

But all I know is that at last my hand crept into Luly's, and in that mutual pressure a rapturous sense of tenderness and contentment came flooding over me. It was thus we returned, still silent, still hand in hand, still giving each other little squeezes, and passed under the roses into the house.

If Fanny had resolved to ask for a divorce after RLS's near-fatal visit to the Santa Lucias to escape the fogs of Monterey, now she had obviously done so. He wrote Sir Sidney Colvin in London: "In coming here I did the right thing; I have not only got Fanny patched up again and in health, but the effect of my arrival has straightened up everything. As now arranged, there is to be a private divorce in January. . . and yours truly will be a married man as soon thereafter as the law and decency permit. The only question is whether I shall be alive for the ceremony." (RLS maintained a steady correspondence with his friends, and he apparently sent much the same message to several people at once. This passage is quoted, with the change of only three or four words, in Swearingen's typeset chronology as having been written to Charles Baxter, a friend from his days at the University of Edinburgh.)

A letter from RLS to Sir Sidney dated October 21 reveals that Fanny and Lloyd had returned to their home in East Oakland to wait out the legal proceedings for the divorce. RLS remained in Monterey two more months. At this point he interrupted his writing of *The Amateur Emigrant* just as the first draft was half finished and took up a novel about the wild and wooly West, which he called, *Arizona Breckenridge*. At least half his fascination with the subject was the, to him, strange names, many with an Indian or Spanish base, that he loved to pronounce over and over again. He never completed this novel, but while still in Monterey, he did considerable research on the life of Thoreau for an article already promised for *Cornhill* magazine.

While RLS continued to write in what we must assume was a spare and at times cold room at the French Hotel, Fanny made the most of her time waiting out the divorce. She often visited Joe and Belle in San Francisco, where Joe shared a painting studio with Jules Tavernier. Fanny and Belle resumed the art lessons they had started in Paris by enrolling, with Joe's recommendation, in classes conducted by another artist, Virgil Williams. Virgil and Dora Williams became firm and helpful friends of Fanny, and later of RLS as well. She also met, once, a literary figure from England, Oscar Wilde, who attended a tea at Joe's studio. Through the Williamses, she also met Bret Harte, who apparently read some of her writing and encouraged her. I can find no reference that RLS later met with this American author as well.

In Monterey, RLS's "family" was now almost exclusively to be found within the confines of Jules Simoneau's restaurant. "In my little restaurant at Monterey," he wrote in *The Old Pacific Capital*, "we have sat down to table day after day, a Frenchman, two Portuguese, an Italian, a Mexican, and a Scotchman: we had for common visitors an American from Illinois, a nearly pureblood Indian woman, and a naturalized Chinese; and from time to time a Switzer and a German came down from country ranches for the night."

When RLS was not at the restaurant, in his room writing, or visiting one of the many people who befriended him, he was walking, hiking, we might say, for he loved to walk not only along the sandy edge of Monterey Bay, but up the slopes as far as what is called today Jacks Peak. Highway 1 runs over a lower shoulder of this peak connecting Monterey and Carmel with a four-lane highway where there was once the "dusty road" to the Mission that Nellie Van de Grift Sanchez described in her account of her brother-in-law's visit to Carmel. Walking, hiking, climbing all were quite natural to a Scotsman, even one with weak lungs. He wrote:

But the sound of the sea still follows you as you advance, like that of the wind among the trees, only harsher and stranger to the ear, and when at length you gain the summit [Jacks Peak, this would have been] out breaks on every hand and with freshened vigor that same unending, distant rumble of the ocean; for now you are on the top of the Monterey peninsula, and the noise no longer only mounts to you from behind along the beach towards Santa Cruz, but from your right, also, round by China-town and the Pinos light-house, and from down before you to the mouth of the Carmello River. . . .

At sunset, for months together, vast, wet, melancholy fogs arise and come shoreward from the ocean. From the hilltop above Monterey the scene is often noble, although it is always sad. The upper air is still bright with sunlight; a glow still rests upon the Gabelano Peak [today called Fremont Peak, the highest point of the Gavilans] . . . but the fogs are in possession of the lower levels; they crawl in scarves among the sand-hills; they float, a little higher, in clouds of gigantic size and often of a wild configuration; to the south, where they have struck the seaward shoulder of the mountains of Santa Lucia, they double back and spire up skyward like smoke. Where their shadow touches, color dies out of the world. The air grows chill and deadly as they advance.

The forest RLS wandered through each time he sought out Jacks Peak is called Del Monte Forest today. Pebble Beach is located within its confines and so is a private school called the Robert Louis Stevenson School. Both the sylvan setting and the reason the school was named after him would have pleased RLS greatly. At a very special gathering of the school's faculty and students during the first week of June, 1965, Jules Simoneau's daughter, Josephine Fussell, was the speaker. Mrs. Fussell, who died in 1973 at the age of 96, admitted that she was only 2 years old when RLS was in Monterey, but she had been raised on her father's stories about the frail Scotsman and she related many of these accounts. Then, to close the program, the reason for choosing RLS's name for the school was explained by Robert U. Ricklefs, the school's founder and now its president emeritus: some 100 names had been suggested, and these were culled away until only two were left, RLS and Sir Francis Drake. RLS's name won out, Mr. Ricklefs related, because of his "historic relation to the Monterey region, but mainly because of his contribution to English literature and the art of writing."

The "deadly fogs" of the Monterey Peninsula are usually gone by the time RLS arrived there; the Peninsula's "summer" is usually late September through the end of November. Some years, however, these fogs have persisted into Thanksgiving week, and perhaps this was one of them. "Monterey is curtained in for the night in thick, wet, salt, and frigid clouds," he wrote. The fog finally drove him from Monterey. . . but it must also be suspected that he was urged on by the prospect of being 125 miles closer to Fanny. The "decent" wait for the divorce was an almost intolerable strain on him.

The December 16, 1879, issue of the *Monterey Californian* carried an article called "Hidden Treasure" attributed to RLS. The experience that resulted in it probably prompted what was to become his first famous novel for boys. It appears it was on this date that he collected his final $2 from Editor Bronson, still unaware of where the money really came from, then boarded the little train that would take him to San Francisco.

The Old Pacific Capital closes with his final assessment of a place he had come to love despite the misery the constant fog imposed on him. He had written articles for the newspaper about the new railroad and its new station. The purpose of that new railroad was to serve a new hotel – the first of several to be named Hotel Del Monte, as was the one that arose from the ashes of the previous structure, the final one of which is today government property utilized as the U.S. Naval Postgraduate School. Wrote RLS:

The Monterey of last year exists no longer. A huge hotel has sprung up in the desert by the railway. Three sets of diners sit down successively to table. Invaluable toilettes figure along the beach and between the live oaks; and Monterey is advertised in the newspapers, and posted in the waiting room at railway stations, as a resort for wealth and fashion. Alas for the little town! it is not strong enough to resist the influence of the flaunting caravanserai, and the poor, quaint, penniless native gentlemen of Monterey must perish, like a lower race, before the millionaire vulgarians of the Big Bonanza.

7
SAN FRANCISCO

RLS WROTE HIS FRIEND
Colvin in a letter from San Francisco dated December 26: "For four
days I have spoken to no one but my landlady or landlord, or to restaurant waiters. This is not a gay way to pass Christmas, is it? . . ."

If RLS thought his move from Monterey would bring him more
constant contact with his beloved, he was wrong. When his letters
arrived in Great Britain they caused a storm among his friends because they thought Fanny was treating him callously, allowing him
to languish unattended during the holiday season. He may have had
some inner hopes, but basically he knew that their relationship had
to remain casual for a while longer. His strict upbringing and sense of
what was proper—whether he as the rebellious young writer
thought it was fair or not—made him understand that Fanny did
have a son, daughter, and possibly an ex-husband to "make" Christmas for. In due time, they enjoyed "dates" of sorts with Lloyd, Belle
and ocasionally Nellie as "chaperons or boon companions."

RLS researcher Anne Roller Issler assures us that the day the
Scottish writer went looking for affordable accommodations—he
had decided to place himself on an even stricter budget than he had

followed in Monterey – he fell upon a landlady who not only mis-trusted "foreigners," but tended to dislike them at sight. RLS knocked at the front door at 608 Bush Street and was greeted by Irish-American Mary Carson. It was then a three-story wooden building of 14 rooms. The building RLS knew has long vanished, but there has been erected at that address a small plaque beside the entrance commem-orating his stay there.

The reason she didn't like foreigners was apparently that they "didn't make good tenants" and often skipped out with several weeks' rent in arrears. RLS's appearance at that time was not very re-assuring to her. He was gaunt to the point of looking like a skeleton with skin stretched tightly over it. As young Lloyd had noted ear-lier, his velvet coat, like the one he wore in his university days and that gave him that nickname, was no longer colorful; it was just plain shabby. When RLS sensed her hesitancy, he opened up to be more friendly toward her, telling her he was a writer and quite frankly there had been times when he could scarcely pay his rent. He was, however, expecting money "momentarily" from London – a phrase he had often used at the Monterey Post Office – and could pay in ad-vance now. Could he see a room?

She took him to the second floor and showed him one. It must have appealed to him, for, unlike his Monterey lodgings, it was at least properly furnished and had a wood stove for warmth. RLS used all his Old World charm in thanking her for allowing him to see the room and promised to let her know his decision soon. He then left, apparently looking about to see what was available at a lesser rate, but finally returned in the evening and paid the first month's rent in advance – $12.

Kevin Starr, in *Americans and the California Dream*, says that the San Francisco of this time was well known to the younger Euro-peans of the Bohemian set as an "in" place. Starr writes that at first San Francisco acquired an enviable reputation as a "breezy" literary frontier, but this eventually collapsed. Those who would associate themselves with creative endeavors had to look in other fields, and painting won out.

Minor artists of European background drifted into town, men who knew the bohemianism of the Continent, and in their exile they recreated so far as possible what they had known in younger days. Studios opened, and in 1871 an Art Association was established under the directorship of Virgil Williams, who had studied in Rome and Paris, which offered instruction for painting to young Californians, preparing the better of them for study in Europe.

Gradually, throughout the 1870s, San Francisco acquired a colony of those pursuing the arts more or less full time, and certainly pursuing *la vie bohème* with enthusiasm. Arriving in San Francisco in 1879, Robert Louis Stevenson came upon this second stage of bohemia and was charmed. Climbing of an afternoon the two flights of stairs leading up to the studio of Jules Tavernier at 728 Montgomery Street, he would be admitted after giving the secret knock which prevented creditors from bursting in upon the almost always broke French painter. Stevenson would throw his reedy body on a sofa to talk and smoke by the hour, or just to watch Tavernier at his easel. . . .

Others would drop by, journalists, actors and actresses from shows in town, painters such as Julian Rix, who kept his own studio nearby, or a group of friends from the newly established Bohemian Club, of which Tavernier was a leading member. . .

Starr tells that RLS was joined at the studio by his friend Charles Warren Stoddard, "poet, essayist and, in a very gentle way, bohemian extraordinary." Stoddard joined Bret Harte and Ina Coolbrith in 1868 "in the editorial leadership of [the] *Overland [Monthly]* during its greatest era."

Stoddard and Tavernier founded the artists' colony at Monterey, then mostly a fair weather thing, but later a permanent part of the Monterey establishment. In the end Stoddard moved to Monterey in 1905 and died there four years later.

RLS did not spend as much of his time in the company of "bohemians" as Starr's account might lead one to believe, but rather the story is an excellent one of the tone of the San Francisco that he knew. These people found RLS witty, an excellent conversationalist and with his cosmopolitan background he mixed well with these people. More frequently, however, he was in his room writing, usually in bed both to keep warm and to conserve his energy.

Mrs. Issler relates that the day after RLS moved into the Carson household, he established regular hours and regular habits that he kept to religiously. He became a familiar sight as he walked from Mrs. Carson's to whichever restaurant he was to patronize that day. Breakfast was usually a 10¢ affair of a roll, butter and coffee at a branch of the Original Pine Street Coffee House, the branch then being located at Fifth near Market Street. He usually had a book with him, invariably a biography for one of the lives he was writing for English magazine publication.

Once again he fell into the French ambience for the main meal of the day. He never re-entered the intimacy he had enjoyed at Jules Simoneau's in Monterey, but he did enjoy both the modestly priced cuisine and the touch of class he felt a French restaurant provided that kept him from crossing that imaginary line where the ordinary paupers dwelt. One thing he refused to be all his life was ordinary.

In the 400 block of Bush Street near Grant Avenue, then known as Dupont, was located Louis Donnadieu's restaurant. One could almost set one's clock at noon when RLS was seen to enter, again with a book under his arm, but this time, Mrs. Issler's research tells us, a French novel. For 50¢ he was able to get a full meal that included wine and a parting brandy, which appears to have been his favorite alcoholic beverage all his life.

RLS would take his time getting home after lunch. He was absorbing the sights and sounds of San Francisco—a foreign city to him—with the intensity of any writer soaking in background against which to weave a story. As it turned out, *The Wrecker* had San Francisco basics, and Mrs. Carson's husband served as a model for a character in the novel. His favorite place of all to observe people was Portsmouth Square, a short walk from his Bush Street address and a place still "teeming with humanity," as many RLS biographers echo the same phrase. A visit there today shows a great variety of people rushing to, from and across the square, under which there is now a parking garage which RLS could not even contemplate during his time. The flavor is definitely Oriental, and the old folk of San Francisco's Chinatown regularly take the sun there, gossip or keep to themselves and read the Chinese newspapers, for the most part printed two blocks up the hill on Grant Avenue.

San Francisco was the first place in the entire world to erect a lasting tribute to RLS. Two prominent San Franciscans of the day, Bruce Porter, artist, and Willis Polk, architect and builder, both in their late 20s, provided money, volunteer work, and materials so that the statue we see there today cost only $1,500 to erect. It was once in the center of Portsmouth Square, dedicated there on October 17, 1897. Among those present at the dedication ceremonies three years after RLS's death were Lloyd, Dora Williams, and Mary Carson. They more than anyone else understood how important this corner of San Francisco had been to the author.

The statue has since been moved to a corner of the square, and in the process the ship *Hispaniola*, which tops the memorial, has changed tacks and points in the opposite direction from that of the day it was dedicated. (The *Hispaniola* was in *Treasure Island*.)

Fanny and her family now gradually came to see more of RLS. The Christmas season was over, and Fanny would take the ferry from Oakland to see the man described flatly by many biographers as "her long-time lover." California law then required a husband to support his wife and children throughout the divorce proceedings. Sam Osbourne was pulling down $10 a day then as a court reporter, and that was an excellent salary. The self-conscious RLS had now imposed greater poverty upon himself, "self-imposed penury" of 70¢ a day, Mrs. Masson wrote. But this did not keep him from enjoying special occasions with Fanny and her brood. It seems that she helped finance some of these outings from her allowance from hubby Sam. And RLS had an intricate mind that probably found a justification for all this. The divorce was close now and RLS and Fanny made no secret that they intended to marry. Even in San Francisco they found much to bind them to each other and ease in entering each other's circle of acquaintances. Both Fanny and Belle had earlier been art students of Virgil Williams. The dinners were usually at French restaurants, which always brought into the conversation their times together at Grèz.

Nellie wrote in *Scribner's Magazine* years later brief but intimate glimpses into RLS's life in San Francisco. Taken together with the other bits and pieces gleaned from other biographers, they fill out nicely the picture of this most unusual and warm human being:

In stories of his San Francisco days there is much talk of the restaurants where he took his meals. The one that I particularly remember was a place kept by Frank Garcia, familiarly known as "Frank's." This place, being moderately expensive, was probably frequented by him only on special occasions, when Fortune was in one of her smiling moods. Food was good and cheap and in large variety in San Francisco in those days, and venison steak was as often served up to us at Frank's as beef, while canvasbacks had not yet flown out of the poor man's sight; so we had many a savory meal there, generally served by a waiter named Monroe, between whom and Mr. Stevenson a friendship founded on mutual respect existed. They now and then exchanged a friendly jest, and I remember one day when Monroe, remarking upon the depression of spirits from which Louis suffered during a temporary absence of women of his family, said: "I had half a mind to take him a piece of calico on a plate."

Another facet of the RLS personality was shown in this recollection by Nellie: "Of all the popular songs of America, he liked 'Marching Through Georgia' and 'Dixie' best. For 'Home, Sweet Home', he had no liking—perhaps from having heard it during some poignant moment of homesickness. He said that such a song made too brutal an assault upon a man's tendrest feelings, and believed it a much greater triumph for a writer to bring a smile to his reader than a tear—partly, perhaps, because it is a more difficult achievement."

Again it seems necessary to stop and wonder for a moment at the relatively short time ago that RLS actually lived in California; I think it is not the fact that it was little more than a century ago, but rather because so many things have happened in that stretch of time that makes 1880 seem almost ancient history. There are, of course, people alive today who were born in the 1880s. There are those who know people who remember people who knew RLS himself. He was not a part of California's remote past, but rather it is that so much has happened to California—and the rest of the world—during that time. History gives us little to wonder at in the 100-year span between, say, 700–800—the century after the death of the historical King Arthur—yet more scientific and technological advances have been made—some mistakenly labeled as progress—in the last 100 years than in the 2,000 years since the birth of Christ. That's why RLS seems to some to come from a distant epoch. Yet Nellie was writing of 1880 when she recalled:

My special memory of him here (in San Francisco) is of many walks taken with him up Telegraph Hill, where the streets were grass-grown because no horse could climb them, and the sidewalks were provided with steps or cleats for the assistance of the foot-passengers. This hill, formerly called "Signal Hill," was used in earlier days, on account of its commanding outlook over the sea, as a signal station to indicate the approach of vessels. . . . When we took our laborious walks up its precipitous paths it was, as now, the especial home of Italians and other Latin people, who dwelt happily on their chosen height and mourned not for sunny Italy, for were not the skies here as blue, the flowers as sweet, and the sea as generous in its yield of fish to the lateen-sailed boats that skimmed across its rippling surface as in the home of their birth?

For some reason, there is among several RLS biographers considerable confusion as to when Fanny actually got her divorce from Sam. Many say it came about in January, 1880; but as Swearingen points out, there is Fanny's certified copy of the divorce, dated December 18, 1879, at the Silverado Museum in St. Helena. This confusion has allowed writers to graze at will in the pastures of their imagination, but it seems they often fed on crabgrass. What appears to be behind the confusion is Fanny's reluctance to get married immediately and the fact that RLS came close to death yet again in January, 1880. Although Fanny wanted to nurse him back to health personally, she at first installed him in a hotel near their Oakland home, not in the home itself.

One explanation of all this is the stern Victorian age in which these events took place. Fanny and her sister, Nellie, were already subjects of gossip because they dared smoke cigarettes. They had struck out alone, and at tender ages, but this was in the era of California's mining towns and camps when a woman was often as not "just one of the guys." It was only in looking back over a quarter or a half century that one cannot understand the restraints of the times to be "respectable." Further, even after the December date, Sam was still making certain that his children and their mother were not without money to spend. In a nutshell, for the moment there was no particular need for a formal wedding. It had been a mutual decision between RLS and Fanny, for the most part out of deference to RLS's parents—who were still not certain a married woman 10 years older than their son was the proper choice as his bride.

It comes out that Fanny had started a correspondence with RLS's mother, a most delicate and diplomatic correspondence that eventually bore fruit. Mrs. Thomas Stevenson found Fanny to be quite acceptable after all—for one thing, Fanny's letters revealed she had allowed that a grown man always retained something of the boy in him, and this boy would always need his natural mother. Butter would have melted on more than the scones that were placed on the table at the Edinburgh home of the senior Stevensons!

Rosaline Masson's 1914 account of RLS still has something of the Victorian touch:

But ill-health, overwork, penury, loneliness, and the great strain of anxiety overpowered the brave fighter. Two months after his coming to San Francisco he was lying at death's door – "pleurisy, malarial fever, and exhaustion of the system."

A mere touch is all that is needed to send fluttering to earth a leaf that has been scorched by sun and nipped by frosts, and yet, frail and yellow, hangs persistently by its stalk. the touch, in Stevenson's case, was supplied by the illness of the little child of his landlord. Stevenson, so passionately devoted to little children, helped to nurse it.

For six weeks in March and April Louis Stevenson lay dangerously ill, and was nursed back to life by the doctor who attended him, and by Mrs. Osbourne.

The "little child of his landlord" was Robbie Carson, age 4, who came down with pneumonia – and survived. RLS may or may not have contracted something from the lad, as the writer took long turns at his side to free the busy Mrs. Carson and her employed husband. RLS was, indeed, devoted to young children and found the same quality in them that his romantic mind found in the fawn, the colt or any other being when it is very young, apparently defenseless and threatened. This was the love that resulted in *A Child's Garden of Verses*, and it was to amuse young Lloyd Osbourne that *Treasure Island* was born.

But the romantic from Edinburgh had been bitterly disappointed in his lack of sales. He had produced little that sold except the biographical sketches already named. His friends, including Editor Henley back in London, all felt he was writing on the wrong track. They saw his writing through the distortion of their disapproval of his move to chase Mrs. Osbourne 6,000 miles across the world, and his mind and therefore his writing style were now changing with maturity, but the letters of criticism they sent to him in Monterey and San Francisco stung him bitterly. There were times when he must have lost faith in himself and his chosen destiny.

RLS's answer to all this was a fancied need to suffer more, a more desolate garret for the writer, a poorer table. And so in January, 1880, he chopped 25¢ off his daily allowance and he wrote to one of his friends in London that his daily food intake weighed some 2 ounces. This, in turn, resulted in a less healthy body, a constitution open to any disease that sought it out. And while he helped to nurse Robbie Carson back to health, he expended his physical resources to the point that he could not get up out of bed and go to a restaurant.

Fanny Osbourne found out about his condition, possibly through Dora Williams, although at this point RLS and Fanny were seeing quite a bit of each other—she usually being the one to make the ferry trip across the bay. Fanny took one look at her ill Scottish lover and on her own had him moved out of Mrs. Carson's rooming house and to a hotel owned by friends, a very short walk from 554 East 18th Street, the address of her home in Oakland.

8
OAKLAND

THE NAME OF RLS'S NEW
residence was the Tubbs Hotel, named for its builder, Oakland
pioneer Hiram Tubbs, Mrs. Issler reports in her biography. She
describes it as "a four-story wooden structure with pillared porticos,
square towers and cupolas, and a dormered roof. It fronted on East
Twelfth Street [formerly] Central Avenue. The beautifully-kept
grounds covered an entire block, a row of young eucalyptus trees
marking the front curb. The semicircular private driveway touched
the entrance steps of the hotel, merging with Fourth Avenue on one
side and Fifth Avenue on the other."

The scenery, however, was not Fanny's most pressing concern. RLS's health was, and she summoned—upon the advice of the
hotel lessee-manager, Alexander Lopez de Leo de Laguna—Dr. William Bamford. RLS was later to credit the saving of his life to "my wife
that is to be, and one Dr Bamford (a name the Muse repels)" in a
letter he wrote to his London friend, editor, poet, and critic, Sir
Edmund Gosse.

Whether the Muse approved or not, Dr. Bamford's office was
close by at 657 East 12th Street. Hotel, doctor and the Osbourne
residence were all chummily close together, and the principal players

of this drama all had ties with one another. Hiram Tubbs's three daughters had been Belle's playmates at school. Alexander de Laguna was a cultured Spaniard who had been born in Paris and later went to the eastern United States, where a doctor advised him to take a long trip at sea to restore his own poor health. He thus sailed around the Horn, ended up in San Francisco and married an Oakland woman who had at one time hoped to become a writer. Although she never accomplished her ambition, she did form a small circle of writer friends who met with her on a basis so regular that one could say she maintained a *salon*.

RLS suffered what appears to have been his most serious hemorrhage yet while at Tubbs and Dr. Bamford ordered him to lie effortless for 6 weeks. Once he said that RLS could be moved, Fanny finally brought him into what was, after all, her home; Sam Osbourne had bought it in her name some 10 years before. The move came early in April, and finally a wedding date was set: May 19.

"Fanny Osbourne married Louis not expecting he would live, but hoping by her devotion to prolong this life now so dear to her," Belle later wrote in her own autobiography. "Though she admired his work she had no idea he would ever become famous."

Before the formal marriage took place, however, there was a convalescence of several weeks at Fanny's home. Some biographers insist that Sam Osbourne still had some control over Fanny's life at this point, but that he did not resent the "sudden" intrusion of RLS. What appears more likely the case, Sam Osbourne was a gentleman who had genuinely been in love with his wife at one time, and although he preferred amorous adventures to firm married life, he still held Fanny in high regard. He had no wish to hurt her. He did, in fact, make the arrangements to secure the honeymoon cottage in Calistoga for Fanny and RLS.

Sam and Fanny had been still teenagers when they were married, and his quasi-military and later quasi-judicial career kept him moving from one place to another. He apparently never lost his dashing appearance, and he enjoyed conquests. He married again after his divorce from Fanny, but he remained an adventurer to the end. He disappeared in 1887 and was never heard from again. What appeared to be his clothing was found at the edge of San Francisco Bay, but the identification was never positive.

Although it is obvious that the illnesses that plagued RLS throughout his life had various causes—the dampness of his childhood home in Edinburgh, the self-imposed poverty he suffered while waiting to be able to support himself by his writing and the bad eating habits this often brought on—his weak lungs were his main disability. There are more biographers of RLS even today who pass off his illness as tuberculosis—he himself had called it consumption, that day's term for TB—than there are who have taken a serious look at his medical history. He did later spend winters in Davos and in Saranac, New York, both under the presumption of seeking a respite from, if not a cure of, tuberculosis. Yet it was RLS himself who had early noted that the cold, dry, clear climates of a severe winter helped him little. What proved to be the most healthy climate for his particular constitution was the open sea, and especially the sea breezes of the tropics.

The fogs of Monterey and San Francisco and Oakland did him great harm, and his body told him that; for this reason he had sought out the clear heights of Monterey's Santa Lucia Mountains, and in this same belief he and Fanny were about to honeymoon in the mountains above Napa Valley.

The two foremost doctors who treated RLS, first at Davos and then at Saranac, never did render a firm verdict of tuberculosis. Many years later, men of medicine studying all the available data on RLS's illness and its records have agreed that it was bronchiectasis. It is explained this way in a chapter by J.C. Furnas in *Stevenson and Victorian Scotland,* edited by Jenni Calder and published in 1981 by the University Press, Edinburgh: "America's great Dr. Edward Trudeau, one of the first to use bacteriology for diagnosis, examined Louis at Saranac and decided that if he ever had tuberculosis, the case was arrested. And some years later an American upper respiratory tract specialist studied the scanty data available and suggested that Louis' trouble was not tuberculosis but chronic severe bronchiectasis . . . a heavy erosion of the bronchial region."

It seems that it was during the periods when Fanny was truly needed that she was at her strongest. Both RLS and his intended bride were subject to swift changes of mood. They would dwell in fits of depression, but usually not at the same time. Much has been made of Fanny's "fits" and other psychotic reactions. At least one biographer suggests that after they were married, RLS found need to shut her away in the bedroom so visitors would not see her when she had become completely unstrung. When in these moods, she would become completely withdrawn from the real world and live in her own.

During their Oakland period, Fanny's strength came forth and, as her sister, Nellie, wrote: "When I recall the sleepless care with which Mrs. Stevenson watched over him at that critical point in his life, it seems to me that it is not too much to say that the world owes it to her that he lived to produce his best works."

Nellie also noticed RLS's deep depressions and wrote of his thoughts while they were all at Oakland:

Brave as his spirit was, yet he had his dark moments when the dread of premature death weighed upon him. It was probably in such a mood that he wrote a poem called "Not Yet, My Soul," an appeal to Fate in which he expressed his rebellion against an untimely end:

> Not yet, my soul, these friendly fields desert,
> . . .
> The ship rides trimmed, and from the eternal shore
> Thou hearest airy voices; but not yet
> Depart, my soul, the unfoughten field, nor leave
> Thy debts dishonored, nor they place desert
> Without due service rendered. For thy life,
> Up, spirit, and defend that fort of clay,
> Thy body, now beleagured.

While RLS's sails were trimmed in Oakland, he obviously benefited from the most devoted care he could have received anywhere in the world outside his parents' Edinburgh home. He responded slowly and was finally at the point where he could receive visitors, although he could not yet hold a pen and write for the hours he would need to produce a story. From across San Francisco Bay came his friend Charles Stoddard, who introduced RLS to the writings of Herman Melville. Stoddard lent him his copies of *Omoo* and *Typee*, and this was his introduction to the South Seas. This fascination would dominate the last years of his life.

It was also during April in Oakland that RLS's finances started to come together. As noted, most of the poverty he seemed to delight in writing home about and telling his new-found chums about was, in fact, self-imposed. Much is made of the fact that once the magic of Fanny's letters to Mother Stevenson had worked their ways, and once RLS firmly announced a wedding date, the question of his chasing after a divorcee did not seem so monstrous, even in the Victorian world. Margaret Stevenson at this point sent her son a cable, in agreement with her husband, "Count on two hundred and fifty pounds annually."

RLS greeted this news ecstatically and wrote off to his London friends that he was no longer penniless, that he had an annual allow- ance—actually, an advance against his inheritance. At first brush this might seem to contradict the argument that he deliberately made himself poor because he was determined to be a writer and live only off his income as a writer. However, it is obvious that in Oak- land this dawned upon him as a too unrealistic decision, even for a romantic such as RLS. He was now about to have a wife and stepson to support.

Further, he was not exactly penniless. He had some money in the bank, acually in the hands of an accounting firm in London, Mitchell & Baxter. Swearingen has chronicled that RLS cabled for several withdrawals and in all received £2,000 from London during his year in California. This was when the pound was worth $5, when $5 was a good sum of money; a meal in a French restaurant in San Francisco then cost 50¢, as RLS well knew.

RLS had been saddled with his "romantic" poverty long enough. Although he and his wife had to count their money care- fully for almost a year yet, they were never in danger of being com- pletely penniless. And RLS's articles were not his only source of income during the California experience. Mother Stevenson wrote him often, usually enclosing a guinea note.

While recuperating at Oakland, RLS wrote the first draft of *Prince Otto*, and he wrote some poems that later were published as a collection under the title *Underwoods*. In the dedication to *Prince Otto*, he described the house Fanny shared with him as "far gone in the respectable stages of antiquity, and which seemed indissoluble from the green garden in which it stood . . ."

Fannie again gives the reporter's eyewitness account: "This cottage was of the variety known as 'cloth and paper,' a flimsy con- struction permitted by the kindly climate of California, and on win- ter nights, when the wind blew in strongly from the sea, its sides

ROBERT LOUIS STEVENSON AT THE TIME OF HIS WEDDING
IN SAN FRANCISCO, 1880.

Robert Louis Stevenson in California

puffed in and out, great to the amusement of the 'Scot', accustomed as he was to the solid buildings of his native land."

Although RLS did some writing in Oakland, it was not in his own hand. Nellie relates: "Every day he worked for a few hours at least, one of us acting as amanuensis in order to save him the physical labor of writing."

I learned the word "amanuensis" from the writings of both Fanny and Belle, and for some reason I found it a delightful word. I at first assumed it meant "Girl Friday," which is now also archaic. It means, simply, secretary—a person taking dictation and writing by hand.

RLS regained his health to the point that Dr. Bamford told him he should now start to get up and about and do some exercise. Nellie relates that the speed with which he took these orders alarmed Fanny; it had been one thing while RLS was dictating from the confines of his bed, but now: "While engaged in dictating he had a habit of walking up and down the room, his pace growing faster and faster as his enthusiasm grew higher. We feared that this was not very good for him, so we quietly devised a scheme to prevent it without his knowledge by hemming him in with tables and chairs, so that each time he sprang up to walk he sank back discouraged at the sight of the obstructions."

During this Oakland period, Swearingen has deduced that young Lloyd was not present, except, perhaps, for brief holidays. He was, the San Francisco Stevenson scholar says, attending school in Locust Grove, Sonoma, and he did not join his mother and new stepfather until after they had gone north to Silverado country. Meanwhile, the friends of Fanny and RLS were busy doing what they could to help make arrangements for the wedding and the honeymoon. Virgil and Dora Williams were most closely associated with this endeavor, and somewhere in the background, several have written, there was Sam himself. The arrangements he had for them were too expensive, however, and they remained at his choice of honeymoon cottage only briefly.

As the date for the wedding approached, RLS's health improved to the point that he and Fanny were able to make several social outings. In fact, the state of his health had had a great deal to do with settling on the date some three weeks before. About a week before the marriage, the happy couple and Nellie went to San Fran-

FANNY OSBOURNE STEVENSON AT THE TIME
OF HER MARRIAGE TO RLS.

cisco to see Gilbert and Sullivan's *The Pirates of Penzance* under the fabled direction of Richard D'Oyly Carte himself, and Nellie records that "Louis said the London 'bobbies' were true to life."

May 19 arrived, and about the only flaw to the occasion that can be found is that the minister spelled RLS's Louis as "Louise" on the marriage registry. He more than made up for this gaffe by having the gentility to describe Fanny as "widowed."

Several accounts of the marriage itself have appeared from time to time, with variations probably caused by time-dimmed memories. To set the record straight, Swearingen quotes the best source possible, Fanny herself, as contained in a letter she wrote to the acknowledged premier biographer of RLS, his cousin, Graham Balfour. He received the letter on May 16, 1901:

Let me make it perfectly clear. On the 19th of May (I forget the year) I went *alone* – no Nellie and no Lloyd – across the bay. At the wharf I met Louis and Mrs Williams. We three, and no one else with us proceeded to the house of the reverend Dr. Scott. Dr. Scott received us in his drawing room and sent for Mrs Scott. There were then present *Dr. Scott, Mrs Scott, Mrs Williams, Louis* and *me*, and a *cat* that had followed Mrs Scott into the room, no other living creature was there. There would have been no-one but the Minister, Louis and me, but two witnesses were required. Mrs Scott and Mrs Williams were the two witnesses.

We then, Mrs Williams, Louis and I went to the Viennese Bakery (a good restaurant in those days) and dined, we three and no more. From the bakery we went to the Palace hotel where we stayed two days, still seeing nobody we knew but Mrs Williams until we started for the mountain; Nelly then brought Lloyd to us, also one dog named ChuChu. Louis, Lloyd, ChuChu and I then went off to St. Helena Mountain by way of Calistoga.

For a number of reasons, it still appears that 12-year-old Lloyd did not accompany his mother and stepfather at the very beginning of their honeymoon retreat. Because his school was in nearby Sonoma, it must be assumed that after a brief postwedding meeting with his mother and beloved "Luly," he went off to finish the remaining days of that semester at his school, then joined the couple.

RLS himself had sought out a Presbyterian minister to perform the rites and had found Dr. William Scott at his home at 521 Post Street. The marriage was performed in the parlor of that address.

9
NAPA VALLEY

RLS WROTE HIS FRIEND,
Sir Sidney Colvin, the week before his marriage: "Whenever I get
into the mountain, I trust I shall rapidly pick up. Until I get away
from these sea fogs and my imprisonment in the house, I do not hope
to do much more than keep from actual harm."

This precisely explains why Fanny consulted so closely with
their friends, the Williamses, about a suitable honeymoon site. RLS
had already drawn from his London account, his parents had sent
more money, and now they wanted to get a complete change of scenery—a change that would allow RLS to build himself back up to the
point where he would have the strength to take his bride and stepson back to Scotland and to present them to his parents.

Virgil Williams was already at their country home near Calistoga. He was preparing for the new term at his California School of
Design, which was to begin May 17. It was because of this that Dora
Williams stayed behind in San Francisco alone to be with Fanny;
Virgil would not be denied his time in the country, and, besides,
planning a wedding and a honeymoon of this sort was strictly "girls'
work." Virgil missed the marriage ceremony, and because he had returned to San Francisco to open the school, he also missed seeing the

Stevensons at Calistoga. Yet there survive today some stories that RLS and Fanny were guests of the Williamses at Calistoga . . . simply because there was considerable talk in the sparsely populated region at the time that Virgil and Dora were preparing for company that May at *their* place. This was never true. Stevenson himself has mentioned them in his Silverado writings, but this appears to be a way of thanking them for all time for their help and not for historical accuracy. As we will soon see, RLS changed the names of most of the real people he dealt with and otherwise had his own peculiar way of dealing with the Silverado experience.

In picturing mentally the area RLS was now about to visit, thanks to investigations made by Dora Williams and Fanny, it must be remembered that 100 years ago California was still a new land. The valleys and hills north of San Francisco Bay were opening up to settlers of all types, including the pioneering wine families from Europe. It was, in many ways, a land something like the England of yet 100 years earlier, that is, the 1700s. There were *bandidos* in California and highwaymen in England and stage coach transportation in both. California in the late 1800s was a country that would automatically trigger the romantic mind of the likes of RLS. It must be seen throughout his own writings of this time in his life, as well as the writings of others about him, that he never stopped playing games, never stopped seeing how far he could go with the smallest experience in this—to him—foreign land. How much could he get out of every moment?

The California Pacific Railroad was the obvious means of transportation, 68 miles from San Francisco to Calistoga by way of Vallejo. Today a drive up Napa Valley is a peaceful experience, with town namesigns along the way pretty much the same today as they were then. After crossing into Napa County from either the Golden Gate Bridge and Marin County or by way of Berkeley and thence Vallejo, today's motorist arrives at Napa, and the town signs follow every few miles just the way they read in the railroad timetable in effect when RLS and Fanny journeyed there: Yountville, Oakville, Rutherford, St. Helena, Calistoga. Calistoga was the end of the line, and the railway station is there today, preserved as a State Historic Monument and looking on the outside exactly as RLS would have remembered it.

The Stevensons could leave San Francisco late in the afternoon of May 22, after their honeymoon at the old Palace Hotel, and make the complete trip the same day. The 4 P.M. departure would have given them part of the ride up Napa Valley after dark, however, and Swearingen concludes that the newlyweds decided to stay overnight in Vallejo for the sole reason that they wanted to travel up the Valley in daylight.

They stayed at the Frisbie House, a hostelry RLS spelled "Frisby," with his unexplainable disregard for accuracy in names. On the other hand, he may just have been getting his revenge for a not-so-pleasant stay. The long-disappeared hotel was then located near Mare Island Strait and, from its position at the northeast corner of Second Street and Lemon Avenue in South Vallejo, had a partial water view. Here is how RLS described the scene in *The Silverado Squatters*:

The Frisby House, for that was the name of the hotel, was a place of fallen fortunes, like the town. It was now given up to laborers, and partly ruinous. At dinner there was the ordinary display of what is called in the west a two-bit house: the tablecloth checked red and white, the plague of flies, the wire hencoops over the dishes, the great variety and invariable vileness of the food and the rough coatless men devouring it in silence. In our bedroom, the stove would not burn, though it would smoke; and while one window would not open, the other would not shut. There was a view on a bit of empty road, a few dark houses, a donkey wandering with its shadow on a slope, and a blink of sea, with a tall ship lying anchored in the moonlight. All about that dreary inn frogs sang their ungainly chorus.

The next day was better. The train departed at 9:10 A.M. and took them first through "bald green pastures."

The sun shone wide over open uplands, the displumed hills stood clear against the sky. But by-and-by these hills began to draw nearer on either hand, and first thicket and then wood began to clothe their sides; and soon we were away from all signs of the sea's neighborhood, mounting an inland, irrigated valley. A great variety of oaks stood, now severally, now in a becoming grove, among the fields and vineyards. The towns were compact, in about equal proportions, of bright new wooden houses . . . sun sparkling on clean houses.

This pleasant Napa Valley is, at its north end, blockaded by our mountain. There, at Calistoga, the railroad ceases, and the traveller who intends faring farther, to the Geysers or to the springs in Lake County, must cross the spurs of the mountain by stage. Thus, Mount Saint Helena is not only a summit, but a frontier; and up to the time of writing it has stayed the progress of the iron horse.

From the Calistoga railroad stations they had but a short carriage ride to their next destination, the Springs Hotel. This, they both knew, would be their last taste of luxury for some months to come. The reason for their trip, after all, was to get away from the sea fogs and get up into the clear air that seemed balm to RLS's lungs. The floor of Napa Valley knows fog, but the mountaintops around it were high above these intrusions.

The town of Calistoga itself had been founded only 23 years before the Stevensons arrived. The name speaks of the dreams its founder, Samuel Brannan, had: It is a combination of California and the resort for the wealthy in New York, Saratoga. The area has a number of hot springs and geysers that were well known to the Indians whose province this area formerly was. They enjoyed bathing in the waters and no doubt believed, as did the white man who came later, that it was beneficial to the health.

Brannan was one of those remarkable California success stories who had big dreams and then lived them. He was born a downeast Yankee from Maine who originally came West in 1846 when the West was being won from Mexico. He had a newspaper in San Francisco, a merchandising concern in Oakland, and did extremely well in his dealings with the gold prospectors and the land speculators. He built the Calistoga Hot Springs Hotel, where RLS and Fanny were to spend a few days. His memory is recorded in a large plaque today at the site of the original hotel, which burned three years after the Stevensons departed but was rebuilt.

Brannan not only built the luxury hotel, but persuaded other entrepreneurs to establish in the area, thus both supporting his enterprise and building a community. Mrs. Issler rightly laments in *Our Mountain Hermitage* that RLS never knew the man, for, as she points out, RLS preferred to write about people and use travel only as a backdrop for personalities.

Open weekends at Calistoga is the Sharpsteen Museum and Sam Brannan Cottage, which offer scenes of Calistoga's founding days, a sculpture of RLS and Fanny, and the cottage they are believed to have stayed in, spared by the fire.

Before firming up their plans for the mountaintop stay, the Stevensons (there is yet no mention of Lloyd being with them) took in the local sights. Napa Valley remains as enchanting an area today as it appears to have been then, and it invites leisurely exploration. RLS and his bride took a horse and carriage and another individual who was either a hired guide or, with RLS's easy way of winning friends, perhaps a volunteer acquaintance, to search about the hills and valleys of the region. After two hours, they ended up at what is known even today as the Petrified Forest. The proprietor of this geo-logic marvel impressed RLS even more than the "forest" itself, and both have been immortalized in his writings.

Today the Petrified Forest is about a 20-minute drive from Calistoga, west on Petrified Forest Road, up the sides of rather steep hills with winding roads that from time to time afford a spectacular view of Mount Saint Helena, just as RLS described them in *The Sil-verado Squatters*. I don't know what I expected, after hearing about a petrified forest since childhood, and apparently neither did RLS. In both our cases, our initial reaction was disappointment. I can explain mine only in that to me a "forest" is something that stands upright. I was somehow unprepared for the Sequoias-turned-stone flat on the ground, some in fragments, some tremendous logs not yet com-pletely excavated. It took only a few minutes of poking around, how-ever, to understand the fascination of the place.

Wrote RLS: "And the forest itself? Well, on a tangled, briery hillside—for the pasture would bear a little further cleaning up, to my eyes—there lie scattered thickly various lengths of petrified trunk, such as the one already mentioned. It is very curious, of course, and ancient enough, if that were all. Doubtless the heart of the geologist beats quicker at the sight; but, for my part, I was might-ily unmoved. Sight-seeing is the art of disappointment."

It is interesting to note that the sentence that starts "Doubt-less the heart . . ." is often quoted, but it is always cut off at the semi-colon. RLS considered the forest secondary to the man who opened it up and who was then the proprietor. Because he was more people oriented than I, he found this character more fascinating in his scheme of things. This man has gone down in literature as Petrified Charley because that's how RLS referred to him. On the grounds of the Forest there is a beautifully-executed plaque commemorating RLS's visit there, showing in bas relief RLS and "Charley" himself.

RLS wrote: ". . .we came on a huge wooden gate with a sign upon it like an inn. 'The Petrified Forest. Proprietor: C. Evans,' ran the legend. Within, on a knoll of sward, was the house of the proprietor, and another smaller house hard by to serve as a museum, where photographs and petrifications were retailed."

The scene is much the same today, except we know that C. Evans's real name was Charles Peterson, and no explanation has been offered about the change of name. RLS describes him as "a brave old white-faced Swede." He says Petrified Charley was a seafarer who eventually came to California, "bent double with sciatica, and with six bits in his pocket and an axe on his shoulder." He came upon this bit of California property and told RLS it was "the handsomest spot in the Californy mountains. Isn't it handsome, now?" And to boot he found this fallen redwood forest turned to stone. RLS records that Petrified Charley charged 50¢ per person admission. Today the price is only $2, a remarkable stay in price when compared with escalations in other areas that have taken place during the same time.

When RLS asked his host-guide who had first discovered the forest, RLS records that Charley answered: "'The first? I was that man,' said he. 'I was cleaning up the pasture for my beasts, when I found *this*'—kicking a great redwood, seven feet in diameter, that lay there on its side, hollow heart, clinging lumps of bark, all changed into grey stone, with veins of quartz between what had been the layers of wood."

The recumbent forest is the result of a blast, believed to have occurred more than six million years ago, from Mount Saint Helena when it was a living volcano. This mountain should not be confused with Mount Saint Helens in Washington, which erupted at the beginning of 1980. They were both apparently examples of the same type of volcanic eruption, not mountainside rivers of lava descending to burn and crush everything below, but rather starting with a pyroclastic blast when the volcano became "unplugged," sending out great concussion waves that leveled everything for miles around, followed by minor lava activity. Who can forget the photographs of the forest at the base of Mount Saint Helens, the trees stripped bare and laid flat? This, then, is what had happened farther south in California at Mount Saint Helena; when this happened, however, there were no lumbermen to go in and salvage what timber they could. "Petrified Charley" found the remains of Mount Saint Helena's activity and turned it into a visitor attraction.

The Stevensons had still a few days before they started the search that took them to the remains of the mined-out shaft called Silverado in his search for health and quiet. RLS had known the wines of the Continent even before his university days, and his travels through France—the South of France had been a refuge his parents had sent him to for relief for his lungs—gave him the world's most famous grapes. Subsequent travels throughout France and elsewhere had increased his awareness of the fine points of wine, as well as something of the vintner's craft. When he left Europe, he was under the impression that the great vineyards of France were being destroyed by phylloxera (a plant lice, or aphid) and he seemed to believe the world's only hope lay in the vines of California and Australia.

It was only natural that, being in Napa Valley, RLS would want to visit some of the local vineyards. He did so in the company of a couple he identifies in correspondence only as "young Mr. Johnson, his young wife," along with Fanny. His companions are not mentioned in *The Silverado Squatters*, and his chapter on the wine country rather makes it sound as though he visited the wineries all in one day. Actually, it took at least two occasions, traveling down today's Highway 29 toward St. Helena for two miles, then a sharp jog right (westerly) up Schramsberg Road. Here were located two of the earliest wineries, Alta, founded by C.T. McEachran (RLS spells it M'Eckron) in late 1878, and a little beyond, Schramsberg Vineyards, established by an immigrant German barber named Jacob Schram in 1862. Both vineyards still produce excellent wines. Both may be visited today by telephoning in advance.

Although the Stevensons visited the Alta Vineyards one day and Schramsberg a second day, his account is combined into a single chapter that reveals an educated palate:

Wine in California is still in the experimental stage; and when you taste a vintage, grave economical questions are involved. The beginning of vine-planting is like the beginning of mining for the precious metals: the wine-grower also "prospects." One corner of land after another is tried with one kind of grape after another. This is a failure; that is better; a third best. So, bit by bit, they grope about for their Clos Vougeot and Lafite. These lodes and pockets of earth, more precious than the precious ores, that yield inimitable fragrance and soft fire . . . bide their hour, awaiting their Columbus. . . . The smack of California earth shall linger on the palate of your grandson.

He was not ready to concede that Napa's wines were as great as France's, but he had confidence.

His description of his trips up Schramsberg Road sounds only a little more primitive than it would today:

A Californian vineyard, one of man's outposts in the wilderness, has fea-tures of its own. . . . We visited two of them, Mr. Schram's and Mr. M'Eckron's, sharing the same glen.

Some way down the valley below Calistoga, we turned sharply to the south and plunged into the thick of the wood. A rude trail rapidly mounting; a little stream tinkling by on the one hand, big enough perhaps after the rains, but already yielding up its life; overhead and on all sides a bower of green and tangled thicket, still fragrant and still flower-bespangled by the early season . . . through all this, we struggled toughly upwards, canted to and fro by the roughness of the trail, and con-tinually switched across the face by sprays of leaf or blossom.

RLS described Alta briefly: "Mr. M'Eckron's is a bachelor establish-ment; a little bit of a wooden house, a small cellar hard by the hill-side, and a patch of vines planted and tended single-handed by him-self." And he notes how pleased he was that this fellow Scot, from Greenock, spoke "a word or two of Scotch with him.

Of the other visit: "Mr. Schram's, on the other hand, is the old-est vineyard in the valley, eighteen years old, I think, yet he began a penniless barber, and even after he had broken ground up here with his black malvoisies, continued for long to tramp the valley with his razor. Now, his place is the picture of prosperity: stuffed birds on the veranda, cellars far dug into the hillside, and resting on pillars like a bandit's cave: all trimness, varnish, flowers, and sunshine, among the tangled wildwood."

The very white wooden home, the very veranda are all still there for the visitor to behold, although I don't recall seeing any stuffed birds during my visit. A plaque beside the entrance to the deep cellars recalls RLS's visit. Wrote RLS of his visit there:

Stout, smiling Mrs. Schram . . . entertained Fanny in the veranda, while I was tasting wines in the cellar. To Mr. Schram this was a solemn office; his serious gusto warmed my heart; prosperity had not yet wholly banished a certain neophite and girlish trepidation, and he followed every sip and read my face with proud anxiety. I tasted all. I tasted every variety and shade of Schramsberger, red and white Schramsberger, Burgundy Schramsberger, Schramsberger Hock, Schramsberger Golden Chasselas, the latter with a notable bouquet, and I fear to think how many more. Much of it goes to London—most, I think; and Mr. Schram has a great notion of the English taste.

Somewhere I have seen the exact number of varieties RLS had to taste that day; I now forget whether it was 18 or 21.

The Stevensons also visited the Beringer Brothers' winery at St. Helena. This was established in 1876 by the brothers Jacob and Frederick, who, as brothers, are remembered by another of their wines today, Los Hermanos—they were the "hermanos" (brothers). RLS was there 3 years before the great Rhine House that now dominates the beautiful grounds was built, but he did visit the same wine cellars behind it that are toured now daily by visitors.

The honeymoon, so to speak, was about over. The proofs for *The Amateur Emigrant* had arrived and needed correcting. And most of all, RLS must find his place above the valley floor to rejuvenate his lungs before all this activity caught up with him once again.

10
SILVERADO

IT WAS MORE THAN
escape from "sea fogs and my imprisonment in the house" that sent
RLS to upper Napa Valley. He explains it this way in *The Silverado
Squatters*:

. . . I suppose there are, in no other country in the world, so many
deserted towns as here in California.
    The whole neighbourhood of Mount Saint Helena, now so quiet
and sylvan, was once alive with mining camps and villages. Here there
would be two thousand souls under canvas; there one thousand or fif-
teen hundred ensconced, as if forever, in a town of comfortable houses.
But the luck had failed, the mines petered out; and the army of miners
had departed, and left this quarter of the world to the rattlesnakes and
deer and grizzlies, and to the slower but steadier advance of husbandry.
    It was with an eye on one of these deserted places, Pine Flat, on
the Geysers road, that we had first come to Calistoga. There is something singularly enticing in the idea of going, rent-free, into a ready-made
house . . .

It soon became apparent to the Stevensons that Pine Flat was much
too far out of the way to serve their purposes. It was also at a relatively low elevation and subject to an occasional fog. And had they

MOUNT SAINT HELENA, WHERE THE SILVERADO
MINE WAS LOCATED.

Robert Louis Stevenson in California

been clairvoyant, they might have foreseen the unforeseeable: during the time they would have been there, a fire leveled the nearly deserted town and would probably have brought them complete personal disaster.

Just in time, RLS fell in with Calistoga's pioneer merchant, name of Morris Friedberg. In his writing, RLS called him Kelmar. . . "That was not what he called himself, but as soon as I set eyes on him, I knew it was or ought to be his name; I am sure it will be his name among the angels."

There was also Mrs. Kelmar, "a singularly kind woman; and the oldest son had quite a dark and romantic bearing, and might be heard on summer evenings playing sentimental airs on the violin." The other son played a flute, and the entire family lived over their store on Calistoga's Lincoln Avenue.

As may be imagined, Kelmar made his living in a variety of ways by serving the needs of the area's population, ways that ranged from money lending to hardware. Somehow RLS came in contact with Kelmar early during his visit at Calistoga, and he commented: "For some reason, Kelmar always shook his head at the mention of Pine Flat, and for some days I thought he disapproved of the whole scheme and was proportionately sad. One fine morning, however, he met me, wreathed in smiles. He had found the very place for me — Silverado, another old mining town, right up the mountain. Rufe Hanson, the hunter, could take care of us — fine people the Hansons; we should be close to the Toll House, where the Lakeport stage called daily; it was the best place for my health, besides. Rufe had been consumptive, and was now quite a strong man, ain't it?"

Mr. Kelmar, of course, was to receive payment for making arrangements, probably in addition to a commission from Rufe. But this did seem to be the best solution, and it was the one the Stevensons accepted.

RLS had often noted Mount Saint Helena towering above the end of Napa Valley at some 4,300 feet. Silverado itself was about 900 feet below the summit. On May 30 the Friedberg/Kelmar family took RLS and Fanny up the mountainside for their first look at Silverado.

It was not a ghost town, but rather an abandoned silver mine and its outbuildings, all rapidly falling into disrepair. What other buildings had been there had now been carried away to other locations – Rufe Hanson's house still bore the sign, Silverado Hotel. Left at the entrance to the mine itself was a ramshackle remain of a building that had been built in three tiers flat up against the mountainside. First level contained the assayor's office; next was the dormitory for the miners; finally there was a top floor of sorts that eventually became Lloyd's private domain.

The glass was out of the windows, as were most of the frames. Holes were in both walls and roof. The ground floor was a shambles of debris, anything from rocks to iron nuts and bolts discarded from long-gone machinery. Neither RLS nor Fanny was discouraged by the sight, however. It managed to appeal to RLS's romantic soul, and Fanny had seen as bad or worse in the mining towns of Nevada where she had lived and made a home as the teen bride of Sam Osbourne.

A mile below Silverado was the Toll House, on a trail over which RLS scrambled down and then back up often. There he found company and men to talk with over the bar when he wanted and emergency supplies such as milk when the hapless Rufe was delayed in making his rounds. As for how RLS could make this precipitous climb so often without giving it a second thought, Ellen Shaffer explained it easily: "He was a Scotsman, and the Scotch are used to walking." It was apparently a matter of will power, not lungs.

The Stevensons returned to Calistoga May 31 and spent more than a week preparing themselves for a stay at the old Silverado mine. Goods were purchased from Kelmar, including white cotton cloth to cover the open windows. Lloyd arrived from his school. RLS worked on proofs and sent off some poems, including "Not Yet, My Soul," which was to be published in *Atlantic Monthly.* On June 9, all three, plus ChuChu, returned to take up residence at Silverado.

Fanny immediately set to making the place a home, and she showed her determination and her skill in doing so. From leather of discarded miners' boots she made hinges so that they had functioning doors. She turned the entrance of the mine tunnel into a refrigerator of sorts, it being cool enough to keep meats and vegetables fresh, and the milk Rufe was to bring up from his place, located a quarter of a mile away, every day.

They had been there only a few days when both Fanny and Lloyd came down with diptheria. RLS took them to Calistoga for treatment and they remained there until June 25. They then remained at their mountaintop hideaway for nearly a full, uninterrupted month.

Uninterrupted? Joe and Belle Strong visited, as did Nellie, while she awaited her own marriage to Adolfo Sanchez. But the effect on RLS was the desired one. His health improved steadily. The place appealed to RLS's sense of adventure at least as much as it did to his 12-year-old stepson, who had brought along his toy printing press and was turning out pages of printed matter, including poems by the man he idolized. Lloyd was rarely separated from his printing press; the following winter, in Davos, Switzerland, RLS wrote poems and illustrated them with wood blocks, while Lloyd turned them out on his little press. Needless to say, in the decades to come these took on a value to collectors that neither RLS nor the boy who used to be called Samuel could ever imagine!

Years later, Belle offered this capsule view of the Silverado period:

. . . They went on their wedding trip to "Silverado," a deserted mine on the top of a high mountain in Napa County, taking Lloyd with them, and a big, foolish, friendly setter dog named "Chu Chu."

Nellie came over and stayed with us [that is, the Strongs, in San Francisco] and a few weeks later we three went to Silverado together. It was a hot trip; the journey by stagecoach up the mountain frightfully dusty, but when we reached the top the air was exhilarating.

The change we found in Louis was amazing; he was like a different man. We found him happily at work on Silverado Squatters and was much cheered by letters from his father and mother who had written most affectionately, sending money and promising a cordial welcome to his wife and step-son if he would come home.

We had our meals out-of-doors and, as there never was a better cook than Fanny Stevenson, they were good ones. She used the mouth of the old Silverado mine for an ice chest and storeroom; there hung sides of venison, pigeons, wild ducks and other game purchased from friendly neighbors and in the chill shadow were cans of fresh milk brought up the mountain each morning.

The "friendly neighbors," of course, were the Hansons, who provided the Stevensons under an apparent contract through Kelmar. RLS was not actually at work on The Silverado Squatters, but rather the journal from which he later wrote. He did complete correcting proofs of *The Amateur Emigrant*, but the actual printing of this was held up, even though RLS had received payment from the publisher. Thomas Stevenson, RLS's father, paid the publisher back because he didn't want the world to know that his son had traveled under such impoverished conditions. The second part of this work, however, did appear during RLS's lifetime in the July and August, 1883, issues of *Longman's Magazine*. The elder Stevenson didn't view the train trip across the United States as demeaning as he did the ocean voyage aboard the *Devonia*.

Nellie seems to be the only one who found no romance at all in the Silverado experience. She wrote: "The old bunkhouse seemed to me an incredibly uncomfortable place of residence. Its situation, on top of the mine-dump piled against the precipitous mountainside, permitted no chance to take a step except upon the treacherous rolling stones of the dump; but we bore with its manifest disadvantages for the sake of its one high redeeming virtue, its entire freedom from the chilling fog which we dreaded for the sick man."

Aside from RLS's own written descriptions, we have only one picture of what the old bunkhouse actually looked like. It is a sketch by Joe Strong, who visited there twice with his wife, Belle. There are three versions of this picture, but the original authentic one is the one verified for me by Miss Shaffer at the Silverado Museum; it is one of two bearing Joe's signature. It shows RLS and Fanny in one of the second-floor rooms. How three versions of this same sketch came into being is told by Arthur W. Orton, whose monograph details his painstaking work in reconstructing the bunkhouse. He writes that this original appears to have been done on the spot, with Strong "working rapidly in pen and ink." The second, Orton states, appears to have been an end-grain woodcut, using Joe's original sketch as its source. The third was either done by Joe from memory, without his first sketch to go by, or by a different artist altogether.

The first version was used as the frontispiece to the first edition of *The Silverado Squatters*, published in 1883 in London by Chatto and Windus. (The most eager readers of this first edition appear to have been the residents of Napa Valley, who now had their first inkling as to the true stature of their 1880 visitor.) Orton says it appears that the London publisher had the copyright on this first sketch; so when the American edition was published in 1884 by

JOE STRONG'S ORIGINAL SKETCH OF RLS AND FANNY AT
WORK WRITING, INSIDE THE SILVERADO BUNKHOUSE.

Roberts Brothers of Boston, a new sketch was prepared from the
first. The third drawing turns Fanny into a much prettier woman
then she ever was, as she sits before a table while RLS is above her,
sitting up in a bunk, writing. By the door, what started off as a rather
indistinct blur in the first sketch now turns out to be a clear-cut cat.

ChuChu the friendly setter would have been mortified! (To me, that first blur looks like a satchel.)

By early July it was obvious that RLS's health had improved to the point where he could hazard the long voyage back to Scotland. The healing was obviously partly psychological, as so much healing really is. Most biographers term RLS's year in California the turning point in his life; this means it was also the turning point in his career as a writer. I once asked a Stevenson scholar if he thought this were true, and he said he doubted it. He thought the transformation was a natural evolution of ability and philosophy. When questioned how RLS's next great work, *Treasure Island*, could be such a break from his past writing and finally propel him to both prominence and prosperity, he replied that the presence of 12-year-old Lloyd had triggered RLS's adventurous imagination and that "any 12-year-old boy could have done it."

To me, the point is obvious: it could have been *any* 12-year-old boy, but it *wasn't*. It was Samuel Lloyd Osbourne. But beyond that, RLS was now a married man and he needed to be a success at his chosen trade. He became that success, and it was because of his California experience. Without California, and therefore without Fanny, RLS may have remained an unsung travel writer. In California he came upon the foreign scenes and the foreign people, all of which jolted him from his rather leisurely approach to life, providing him with fresh material and a mother lode of personalities to populate his stories.

Mrs. Issler puts it well in *Our Mountain Hermitage:* "Stevenson took his marriage very seriously. He had never been self-supporting, and the acquisition of a wife and a family under the conditions existing at the time laid a burden upon his heart and mind, which, together with the breakdown in health from which he never fully recovered, grew at last too heavy to be borne. From then on he was, in all seriousness, writing to earn a living; writing, too, with an interested, able, dictatorial critic by his side."

It is ironic that when RLS was in California, he was an unknown tourist on a romantic mission. Since then, countless people have come forth with half-remembered, often rather impossible memories of having met him. Some very frankly admit they were too young to remember him, but they recount stories they heard from their parents about this penniless Scot with the engaging personality and inquiring mind. For this reason, no one sat down to interview him during the 1879–80 year in California. No one photographed him, although there are several with captions that read, "man on left *may* be RLS." One in Monterey has never been verified. Another, taken at a newspaper office in Calistoga, turns out to have been taken four years after he left.

The Stevenson House in Monterey gives an excellent glimpse of what his surroundings were like when he lived there, and the furniture and mementos of him are authentic, although from a later period in his life.

The Silverado Museum, located on Library Lane, just off St. Helena's main street, which is also Highway 29, has an especially unique collection of material connected with his life. Most of it was purchased from the estate of Austin Strong, the son of Joe and Belle Strong. The museum was founded in 1969 by bibliophile Norman H. Strouse and his wife, Charlotte. He became interested in RLS through his interest in collecting fine books; a fine print edition of *The Silverado Squatters* so intrigued the Strouses that they visited the site of the bunkhouse, now located in Robert Louis Stevenson State Park near the top of Mount Saint Helena. When he retired, they moved to St. Helena. There they set up a foundation to support the museum. They also enticed Ellen Shaffer, who had been rare book librarian for the Free Library of Philadelphia, to take charge as curator.

The bunkhouse itself has long disappeared. As Miss Shaffer says, "It was coming down around their ears when they lived in it." A local civic group, however, did place a mounted tablet of Scotch granite at what is approximately the location of the entrance to the old building to recall RLS's time there.

As for the departure of RLS, Fanny and Lloyd, it came during the week of July, 1880. Nellie wrote: "Then back to San Francisco, where the only memory that remains is that of a confused blur of preparations for leaving—packing, ticket-buying, and melancholy farewells—for he was then homeward bound to old Scotland to introduce his newly acquired American wife to his waiting parents. One day he came in with his pockets full of twenty-dollar gold pieces, with which he had supplied himself for the journey. He thought this piece of money the handsomest coin in the world, and said it made a man feel rich merely to handle it."

RLS, Fanny and Lloyd left San Francisco by train July 29 and arrived in New York August 6. The following day they sailed for Liverpool aboard *The City of Chester* — one year to the day after he had departed Greenock on the Clyde River aboard the *Devonia* for America, California . . . and Fanny.

II
TREASURE
ISLAND

RLS WAS APPROACHING HIS

30th birthday when he returned home. *The City of Chester* put into Liverpool August 17. Waiting to greet them was his erstwhile correspondent, Sir Sidney Colvin, who found RLS looking frail but, for him, in good shape. Fanny looked like her picture, which is as near a noncomment as one can leave behind, and Sam (Lloyd) "colorless."

On the other hand, when they got to Edinburgh, the elder Stevensons welcomed home their only son, his bride and stepson with open arms. Fanny's letters had done their work well.

These two reactions pretty much sum up the way RLS's circle treated his family from then on. The Stevensons were loving and accepting. The London literary circle considered Fanny an outsider, unacceptable both as an outsider and a woman. They continued to resent and resist her for the rest of their lives. This does not mean, however, that RLS and his new family were ostracized. RLS was a genuine friend and a genuine talent, and therefore Fanny was tolerated.

Whatever doubts some critics may have, the California experience left an indelible mark on RLS. Without it, who knows what

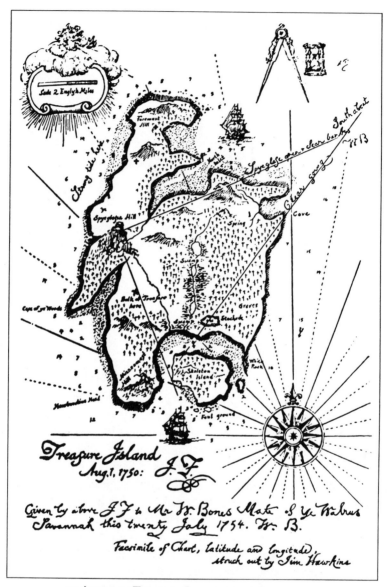

RLS'S MAP OF TREASURE ISLAND HAS MORE THAN A
CASUAL RESEMBLANCE TO POINT LOBOS; SKELETON
ISLAND COULD BE BIRD ROCK, SPYGLASS HILL LOOKS LIKE
BIG DOME, AND CAPE OF WOODS AT THE TIP OF
BIG DOME IS COVERED WITH CYPRESS. THE AREA WITH
THE NOTATION "STRONG TIDE HERE" MAY BE THE
ENTRANCE TO WHALERS COVE.

direction his career may have taken? It was in California where he not only took on the individual who had the most influence on his life thereafter, Fanny, but it was there that his fertile imagination was stirred to the boiling point. He was 100 years too late to know England's highwaymen, but he received firsthand accounts about encounters with Tiburcio Vazquez and Black Bart in Monterey and Calistoga. At Point Lobos, near Carmel, he found a coastline every bit as dramatic as his own Scottish coastline; but perhaps merely because it was foreign, it left a more vital image. In Monterey and San Francisco, he met many of the people who populated such works as *The Wrecker*. And in both Fanny and young Lloyd, he met inspiration.

It took RLS litle more than two months in the Scottish climate before his health again took a turn for the worse. His doctor, a cousin, told him the only way he could survive was to spend his winters in Switzerland. Although this is hardly the life she had planned, devoted Fanny, along with Lloyd, agreed that RLS must go to Davos. It was a bleak and cheerless winter, relieved only the by sessions already referred to concerning Lloyd and his little printing press.

June brought the promise of summer of sorts in Scotland, and the Stevensons took up residence near Pitlochry. The rains kept them indoors for the most part, both RLS and Fanny writing on their own and in collaboration with each other. Needless to say, when RLS's friends learned of this, they reproached him for "lowering" himself. After 2 months they moved to Braemar, now known because it was close to Balmoral, Queen Victoria's summer home, and for a more promising climate. RLS thought of many ways to support his family and even applied for a temporary job as a lecturer at the University. Fortunately, he was turned down.

It was during this period that RLS happened upon young Lloyd as he was drawing imaginary maps of mysterious and distant islands. He picked one up and found Lloyd was enjoying a pastime he himself had loved at that same age. RLS wrote in some place names on the charts, including Spyglass Hill and Skeleton Island and even Treasure Island.

The two minds seemed to lock onto a single track, and Lloyd asked his stepfather if he would make up a story to go with the map —a story less stuffy than some of the adult material the youngster had been forced to hear read aloud.

Thus was born *Treasure Island*, the story that was to change RLS's life. He wrote down chapter after chapter to satisfy the 13-year-old stepson. He first called it, "The Sea Cook," and to make it sound even more dramatic, he started to use a pen name, Capt. George North. It was, however, first published under his own name as an adventure story for boys in *Young Folks Magazine*. It ran in 17 installments from October 1, 1881, to January 28, 1882. He received a total of £30 for it, and the magazine received so much fan mail from young-sters that all concerned were amazed. In 1883, Cassel & Company of London published *Treasure Island* in book form, a cautious total of 2,000 copies, which paid RLS £100.

Meanwhile, the Stevensons had another winter at Davos, and RLS was remonstrated not only by his London friends, but by Fanny as well for "stooping" to writing boys' yarns. It launched him, however, as a world-known author. Collected poetry such as *A Child's Garden of Verses* and short stories also came out of this per-iod, and in January, 1886, *The Strange Case of Dr. Jekyll and Mr. Hyde* was published. "[It] caught the attention of all classes of readers, was quoted from a hundred pulpits, and made the writer's name familiar to multitudes both in England and America whom it had never reached before," quotes Mrs. Masson.

Although neither RLS nor Fanny was good at managing money, *Treasure Island* and *Jekyll and Hyde* (RLS pronounced it "jee-kl") as-sured them that he could, indeed, plan on a life supported by his writing. He was now known, and he was in demand.

Jekyll and Hyde sold an unprecedented 40,000 copies in Eng-land alone during its first 6 months. A great deal more sold in the United States, both in authorized and pirated editions.

Unable to face yet another winter in Davos, RLS decided to return to the United States to winter at Saranac. On May 8, 1887, his father died. RLS took this as a signal that he was no longer bound to the unhealthy climes of Scotland and apparently vowed never to return. He decided that neither the severe winters of Davos nor Saranac really did him much good, but he recalled how the warmer places near the sea — such as the French Riveria — seemed to help. However, it was not the Mediterranean that had his fancy now. He recalled the stories Charles Warren Stoddard had told him of the South Seas during their conversations in Monterey, San Francisco,

and Oakland. He made his decision. He sent Fanny off to San Francisco to charter a yacht.

The season at Saranac ended and he went to New York City,
where he spent an afternoon chatting in Washington Square with
Mark Twain. He lived a month on the New Jersey side of the Hudson River. He was, of course, in the company of his mother, Margaret Stevenson, and their maid, Val (Valentine Roch, of French-
Swiss extraction, who had worked for RLS and Fanny during their
residence in the South of France).

RLS had received £3,000 from his father's will, and his mother
was taken care of for life. RLS was also making money from his writing. This time he was in the New World under considerably differ-

RLS AS CLAN CHIEFTAIN, HEAD OF HIS HOUSEHOLD,
AT HIS FINAL HOME IN VAILMA, SAMOA.
SHOWN IN THE BACK ROW FROM THE LEFT ARE
JOE STRONG, MARGARET STEVENSON,
LLOYD OSBOURNE, RLS, FANNY. IN FRONT OF FANNY IS
BELLE; IN FRONT OF BELLE, HER SON AUSTIN
STRONG. ALSO SHOWN ARE SEVERAL SAMOAN RETAINERS
AND ONE UNIDENTIFIED WHITE GIRL.

ent circumstances: He was in demand. As Fanny searched San Francisco for a yacht and visited old friends, including the Virgil Williamses, her sister, Nellie, and old Jules Simoneau in Monterey, RLS set himself up for further income. He obtained a contract to write 12 articles a year on subjects of his own choosing for *Scribner's Magazine*, at £700 yearly. He made contact with S.S. McClure, who had founded America's first newspaper syndicate in 1884, and obtained agreement to be paid well for a series of letters from the Pacific about his travels.

Then one spring day a telegram arrived from Fanny that the proper yacht had been found. The Stevenson entourage was off almost immediately. The yacht was named the *Casco*, and Mrs. Issler describes it as "a hundred feet long, had two masts, one foresail, one mainsail, two topsails, four jibs and staysails, and was 74 tons burden." Included in the $750 monthly charter price was Capt. Albert Otis and a crew of five. The passengers included RLS, Fanny, Val, Margaret Stevenson and Lloyd, now 20, 6 feet tall, blond, bespectacled and frightfully British in speech. His sister, Belle, writes she hardly recognized him.

On Thursday, June 28, 1888, the *Casco* was towed by two tugs through the Golden Gate and let loose in rough Pacific waters which kept almost everyone, including the Captain, in their bunks for the first three days.

What happened after that belongs in another story: Tahiti, Hawaii, Australia and British, now Western, Samoa. "Home" became Samoa, where RLS built a fine house he named Vailima (Five Waters) and where he became a traditional Scottish head of a clan: his own family and a native entourage of hired help who appear to have worshiped the man they called Tusitala – "Teller of Tales."

That departure from California was the last RLS ever saw of the Golden State. There remains one mystery from his California days . . . or rather, it is assigned to his California days. That is the oft-varied argument as to the inspiration for *Treasure Island*. Those from California say that the real Treasure Island was there; then the argument is split two ways: Point Lobos and Mount Saint Helena. The third argument is that Treasure Island took form on a contrived map from the imaginations of first, Lloyd, and finally RLS.

I cast my vote with the Point Lobos crowd. First, those who have visited Point Lobos, that state reserve of carefully guarded

POINT LOBOS: WAS THIS THE ORIGINAL
TREASURE ISLAND AS REMEMBERED BY YOUNG
LLOYD OSBOURNE AND RLS AS THEY COLLABORATED ON
THE STORY'S MAP? SHOWN HERE IS BIG DOME,
PROBABLY THE ORIGINAL SPYGLASS HILL.

nature that juts out into the Pacific some 4 miles south of Monterey, agree it pretty much resembles the original map—except it is a peninsula, not an island. RLS himself said the inspiration came from no one place, but from several, and he had in mind the pirates of the Caribbean. The Caribbean, however, has no sea lions or other such beasts as described, no pines or cypresses, and RLS himself had never been there. Mrs. Issler makes a not very serious play for Mount Saint Helena, saying its odd shape matches that of Spyglass Hill; but so does Big Dome on Point Lobos, and at a much more reasonable height. Mrs. Mackay writes, without attribution: ". . . the distinctive beauty of the Monterey coast, its forested hills curving down to rocky headlands with live oaks and strange wind-twisted cypresses in the spray. (This shore was later borrowed in part by Stevenson for *Treasure Island*.)"

Daiches also mentions the "scenery of the California coast." Mrs. Issler hedges on her admittedly weak argument in *Our Mountain Hermitage* for Mount Saint Helena by writing in *Pacific Historical Review*, volume 34, 1965, (15 years after writing *Hermitage*): "Both the treasure hunt and the descriptions contributed to the legend, still rife, that Point Lobos is Treasure Island." The legend is a story about a treasure hunt RLS made with a Chinese friend on the Monterey Peninsula and wrote about in the *Monterey Californian*.

RLS wrote to Sir Sidney Colvin in 1884: "The scenery is Californian in part, and in part *chic*." It seems that after RLS's death, half the hills of Scotland were said to resemble Spyglass Hill, and no scholar will today state he has actually found Treasure Island. Scholars tend to be stuffy, and I'll stand up for Point Lobos any day.

RLS died December 3, 1894, not of tuberculosis or any other lung affliction, as everyone had imagined he would, but of a stroke. It came suddenly. His shocked family had less than half an hour to understand what was happening and to make him comfortable.

He was buried Samoan style above ground in a tomb atop Samoa's Mount Vaea, which is still sought out by visitors. Fanny's ashes were placed with him in 1915.

As was his wish, his "Requiem" is on the tomb's tablet:

> *Under the wide and starry sky,*
> *Dig the grave and let me die.*
> *Glad did I live and gladly die,*
> *And I laid me down with a will.*
>
> *This be the verse you grave for me:*
> *Here he lies where he longed to be;*
> *Home is the sailor, home from the sea,*
> *And the hunter home from the hill.*

BIBLIOGRAPHY

In 1981, Ellen Shaffer, curator of the Silverado Museum in St. Helena, California, decided to offer as one of her changing exhibits a display of biographies about RLS, complete with a display card by Ernest Mehew, the English scholar who is considered the world's foremost authority on Stevenson, commenting on the value of each biography. He obliged by making a chronological survey of almost all the biographies that have been published. Miss Shaffer describes Professor Mehew's comments as "shrewd, penetrating and incisive . . . you will likewise be interested in the authors whom Mehew regards, with justification, as the villians in Stevenson scholarship."

There is no room here to publish his entire list, but it is worthwhile to preface my bibliography with some of the comments by a true scholar. Publishers were not always listed, for the most part because the books are no longer available.

Balfour, Graham. *The Life of Robert Louis Stevenson,* 1901. "Still the indispensable biography and, if read with Furnas, it provides all the basic accurate biographical information one needs."

Calder, Jenni. *RLS: A Life Study,* Oxford University Press, New York, 1980. "A disappointing book written with great assurance and knowingness. . . . Unsympathetic to Stevenson's literary achievements. One wonders why she bothered to write the book. Most of the critics have praised it."

Furnas, J. C. *Voyage to Windward*, 1951. "The major biography of Stevenson written with access to all material available to Balfour, plus material he did not see. . . . All subsequent biographies have drawn heavily on it but not superseded it."

Hellman, George S. *The True Stevenson: A Study in Clarification*, 1925. "Hellman is the 'villain' in Stevenson's biography. He dismembered and dispersed Stevenson's notebooks, misunderstood and misinterpreted much of the information therein."

Hinkley, Laura L. *The Stevensons: Louis and Fanny*, 1950. "An interesting book by an enthusiast with some useful insights. The first to identify 'Claire' as Mrs. Sitwell."

Rice, Edward. *Journey to Upolu*, Dodd, Mead & Co., New York, 1974. "A badly written book but has one or two interesting ideas and a few out of the way illustrations." Miss Shaffer adds, "The curator regards it as uncommonly snide."

The foregoing excerpts of Mehew's comments are valuable for a number of reasons, the least of which is not the point that RLS could attract such a variety of critics who both praise him and detract from him.

The following is the bibliography for this book, listing works I considered most helpful in guiding me along RLS's path in California.

Caldwell, Elsie Noble. *Last Witness for Robert Louis Stevenson*, University of Oklahoma Press, Norman, 1960.

Daiches, David. *Robert Louis Stevenson and His World*, Thames and Hudson, London, 1973.

Field, Isobel (Osbourne Strong). *This Life I've Loved*, Longmans, Green and Co., New York, 1937.

Fisher, Anne B. *No More a Stranger*, Stanford University Press, Stanford, California, 1946.

Hamilton, Clayton. *On the Trail of Stevenson*, Doubleday, Page and Company, Garden City, New York, 1915.

Issler, Anne Roller. *Happier for His Presence*, Stanford University Press, Stanford, California, 1950.

Issler, Anne Roller. *Our Mountain Hermitage*, Stanford University Press, Stanford, California, 1949.

Issler, Anne Roller. *Robert Louis Stevenson in Monterey, Pacific Historical Review,* issued quarterly by the Pacific Coast Branch of the American Historical Association, University of California Press, Berkeley and Los Angeles, 1965.

Lee, W. Storrs. *California—A Literary Chronicle,* Funk & Wagnalls, New York, 1968.

Mackay, Margaret. *The Violent Friend: The Story of Mrs. Robert Louis Stevenson,* Doubleday & Company, Inc., Garden City, New York, 1968.

Masson, Rosaline. *Robert Louis Stevenson,* T.C. & E.C. Jack, Edinburgh, 1914.

Orton, Arthur W. *Reconstructing the RLS "Silverado Squatters" Cabin,* private printing, St. Helena, California, 1980.

Osbourne, Lloyd. *An Intimate Portrait of R.L.S.,* Charles Scribner's Sons, New York, 1924.

Rice, Edward. *Journey to Upolu,* Dodd, Mead & Company, New York, 1974.

Sanchez, Nellie Van de Grift. "In California with Robert Louis Stevenson, *Scribner's Magazine,* October, 1916.

Sanchez, Nellie Van de Grift. *The Life of Mrs. Robert Louis Stevenson,* Charles Scribner's Sons, New York, 1920.

Starr, Kevin. *Americans and the California Dream,* Oxford University Press, New York, 1973.

Stevenson, Robert Louis. *The Old Pacific Capital,* Colt Press, San Francisco, 1944.

Stevenson, Robert Louis. *The Silverado Squatters,* Silverado Museum edition, Lewis Osbourne, Ashland, Oregon, 1974.

Swearingen, Roger S. *Robert Louis Stevenson in California—Chronology, 1879–1880,* typescript, Chapel Hill, North Carolina, and San Francisco, revised 1981.

Woolfenden, John. "Treasure Island—Is It on Peninsula?", *Weekend Magazine, Monterey Peninsula Herald,* Monterey, California, October 7, 1979.

INDEX